# The Northwest Passage

~

## Atlantic to Pacific: A Portrait and Guide

**Tony Soper**

Bradt Travel Guides Ltd, UK
The Globe Pequot Press Inc, USA

First edition July 2012

Bradt Travel Guides Ltd
IDC House, The Vale, Chalfont St Peter, Bucks SL9 9RZ, England
www.bradtguides.com
Published in the USA by The Globe Pequot Press Inc,
PO Box 480, Guilford, Connecticut 06437-0480

**British Library Cataloguing in Publication Data**
A catalogue record for this book is available from the British Library
ISBN-13: 978 1 84162 438 9

**Photographs**
*Front cover* top © Andy Stewart/Tips Images: Cape Dyer, Baffin Island
bottom © Brandon Harvey: Summer in the Parry Channel
*Back cover* 'Departure of the travelling parties from *Resolute* and *Intrepid*
4 April 1853' from Belcher, Captain Sir Edward, *The Last of the Arctic Voyages*
(London, 1855, vol 1)

**Cover design** Pepi Bluck, Perfect Picture
**Maps** David McCutcheon
**Project manager** Caroline Taggart

Typeset from the author's disc by Artinfusion
Production managed by Jellyfish Print Solutions; printed in Europe

# CONTENTS

Introduction     1

Opening the passage – a historical timeline     5

The Passage today     43
Pond Inlet to Bellot Strait     48
Bellot Strait to Cambridge Bay     76
Cambridge Bay to Holman     93
Holman to Herschel     105
Herschel to Nome     130

Transits of the Northwest Passage to 2011     141

Selected references     150
Ice information     150
Expedition operators     151
Acknowledgements     151
Photographic acknowledgements     152
Index     153

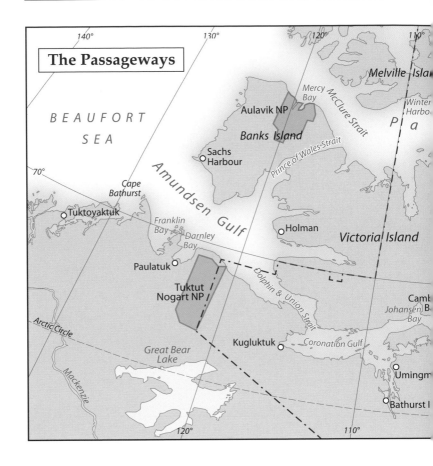

The Passageways

140°   130°   120°   110°

BEAUFORT
SEA

Melville Isla

Mercy
Bay
Aulavik NP

McClure Strait

Winter
Harbo

P    a

Banks Island

Sachs
Harbour

Prince of Wales Strait

70°

Cape
Bathurst

Amundsen Gulf

Tuktoyaktuk

Franklin
Bay
Darnley
Bay

Holman

Victoria Island

Paulatuk

Dolphin & Union Strait

Tuktut
Nogart NP

Camb

Johansen B
Bay

Arctic Circle

Kugluktuk

Coronation Gulf

Great Bear
Lake

Umingm

Mackenzie

120°

110°

Bathurst I

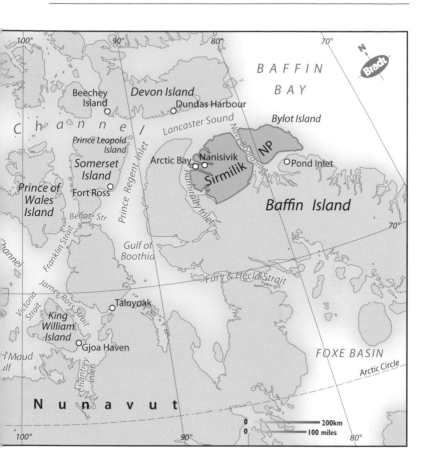

Ah for just one time I would take the Northwest Passage
To find the hand of Franklin reaching for the Beaufort Sea
Reaching one more night to a land so wild and savage
And make a northwest passage to the sea.

Stan Rogers, Canadian folksinger/writer
'Northwest Passage', 1981

*Arctic Canada offers wild scenery and magnificent glaciers, but open water for only a short period every year.*

# INTRODUCTION

Historically, the way to the riches of the Orient for Europeans was by land – the sea route being too long and too stormy. The five-century dream of a trade route to Asia by way of a shortcut from the Atlantic to the Pacific through the Canadian Arctic has only now in the 21st century become a practical reality.

The Northwest Passage threads a series of deep channels that wind the best part of 1,600km through Canada's Arctic archipelago, much of it unsurveyed. It is a summer residence for huge numbers of the world's seabirds, seals and whales, a lot of polar bears and more than enough mosquitoes. It is a permanent home for the hardy hunters who arrived thousands of years ago from Siberia, already adapted to a cruel climate. And from the 15th century to the first decade of the 20th, finding a navigable route through it was a challenge that cost many European sailors their lives.

Bypassing the Panama Canal cuts thousands of kilometres – as much as a third of the distance – from a sea journey between Europe and Asia. Unfortunately, the route lies above the Arctic Circle, encumbered by sea ice and icebergs that clutter narrow waterways between a maze of islands. The labyrinth of ice-choked channels and lack of infrastructure present a near-impossible route for shipping. Before the year 2000, a single sailing vessel and only a very small number of icebreakers

Hanse Explorer *is typical of the ice-hardened motor yachts now able to explore Arctic Canada.*

and ice-hardened vessels had carried travellers through. Yet global warming is having a marked effect and may present an opportunity. Sea ice is a great obstruction to navigation, so reductions in its concentration and thickness encourage maritime activity. In the new millennium it has become clear that the fabled passage is open, possibly for freight, certainly for bold tourists. Even well-found yachts are succeeding.

In the past, the main channel has been navigable only by icebreakers and only for a couple of months each year. Some speculate that as global warming continues this Parry Channel will become a viable transport route. Others say it is unlikely to be an alternative to the Panama Canal for at least a couple of decades. Recent years have seen a marked shrinkage of ice cover in the critical few weeks of high summer, but start and end dates of the opening are unpredictable. Big ships require ports with shore-side facilities, pilotage, emergency services, repair, supply, storage and bunkering, to say nothing of road access across frozen landscapes. At present none of these things exist. On a relatively small scale, freight movements

## Politics and the ice

Opening up the Passage has political implications. Not surprisingly, Canada regards these waters as her own, citing the dominant aboriginal Inuit in support; the existence of a resident population is a key factor in any argument over sovereignty. Currently, ships proposing to transit the passage must report to the Canadian authorities. Other nations, including the US, UK, Denmark and China, claim them for free and unencumbered passage as International Waters, in accordance with the United Nations Convention on the Law of the Sea. As global warming reveals untapped resources of minerals, oil and wildlife, the status of the Canadian Arctic needs to be defined.

*Until recently only icebreakers like I/B* Kapitan Khlebnikov *could transit the Northwest Passage with confidence.*

in Nunavut and the Northwest Territories are pretty much monopolised by the Northern Transportation Company, which has operated above the Arctic Circle since 1934, but even their ice-hardened ships are able to reach the remote hamlets only once a year.

After several earlier transits by icebreaker, I have been fortunate to enjoy the benefits of the easier environment of the last few years. Nowadays it is becoming possible to thread the icy waterways with more conventional expedition ships, those with ice-strengthened hulls. I like to think that the time has come when adventurous travellers will grab the chance of seeing the spectacular Canadian archipelago in a way 16th-century mariners could only dream about.

# OPENING THE PASSAGE – A HISTORICAL TIMELINE

Thousands of years ago the hunter-gatherers of the Siberian coast pioneered to the east across the Bering land bridge to colonise new lands, finding themselves eventually in Greenland. Coming the other way, Irish monks of the seventh and eighth centuries may have been the first Europeans to penetrate high Atlantic latitudes. Sailing sturdy ox-hide curraghs they landed to found communities in the Hebrides, the Faeroes and Iceland, paving the way for a North Atlantic 'stepping stone' passage to North America. The Vikings of Scandinavia were not far behind, exploring and colonising in the ninth and tenth centuries, sustained by plentiful fish and seabirds. Norwegians established permanent colonies in Greenland, subsequently trading with the native groups (historically known as Eskimos) who already inhabited the region, before penetrating southwest to settle in Newfoundland. Then in the 14th century Basque whalers, who had hunted sperm and right whales in the Bay of Biscay, established themselves on the coast of Labrador. British and Dutch fishermen were quick to learn from the Basques and made their way further north.

Mariners were rarely exploring for the love of knowledge

*18th-century whalers worked the Davis Strait for bowheads – the Greenland right whale – much valued because of their reluctance to sink when dead.*

alone: the spirit of curiosity led naturally to the pursuit of monetary gain, with merchants anxious to discover new fishing grounds and more profitable trade routes. The spice trade of the Orient was rich in potential but hard of access. The land routes from Western Europe to 'Cathay' – China – were infested with brigands, difficult and dangerous; the sea route via Cape Horn was long and stormy. British and Dutch adventurers ran the gauntlet of a hostile Spanish South America. Likewise, voyages round the Cape of Good Hope were not only long but monopolised by Spain and Portugal. So there was strong incentive to find a short cut from Atlantic to Pacific, either across the Arctic Ocean – over the top of the world – or along the top of Siberia or Canada. The English called the hypothetical northern route across Canada the 'Northwest Passage'. Either this or a northeast passage – the 'Northern Route' – off the coast of Russia would offer a way to avoid the influence of Spain and Portugal and yet reach the established trading nations of Asia. The prospect of discovering such a valuable route motivated much of the European exploration of the coasts of North America and northeastern Europe.

## FIRST ATTEMPTS

Christopher Columbus sailed west in 1492, on behalf of the Spanish Crown, in search of an economical route to the riches of the East Indies, which were virtually out of bounds eastwards by land for Christian Europe. He found himself in Haiti. Tackling the same challenge, the Italian navigator John Cabot, carrying Letters Patent issued by Henry VII of England but sponsored by the merchants of Bristol, sailed in the caravel *Matthew* in May 1497. He knew that by staying north and taking advantage of the fact that the meridians of longitude converge towards the poles, he would make a 'Great Circle' voyage in high latitudes to the Pacific much shorter. Despite being hampered by a lack of charts, he was probably the first European since the Vikings of the Middle Ages to reach the continent of North America. We are reasonably certain he landed in Newfoundland; maybe he got to Hudson Bay. In 1508–9 his son Sebastian continued the search for a northwestern passage and may have reached the Hudson Strait, between the northern coast of Quebec and Hudson Bay itself. But he certainly got no further.

With no sign of a breakthrough north of Canada, attention turned to the possibility of the Russian route. Sir Hugh Willoughby was sent by the London-based Company of Merchant Adventurers to New Lands to explore the putative Northeast Passage. He sailed in 1553, but his vessel *Bona Esperanza* endured a catastrophic voyage that ended with the entire crew frozen to death on the Murmansk coast. Willoughby's pilot, Richard Chancellor, with *Edward*

*Bonaventure*, survived and found his way to Moscow, where he arranged a trade agreement with Ivan the Terrible. The Muscovy Company was born; a fleet of sealing and whaling vessels fed it with a seemingly inexhaustible supply of Arctic wildlife products and encouraged it to think of trade with the Far East.

*Sir Martin Frobisher, painting by Cornelis Ketel, c. 1577.*

## Frobisher picks up the gauntlet

Possibly as early as 1560 or 1561, the seaman Martin Frobisher planned a voyage in search of a Northwest Passage trade route. But it was not till 1566 that Walter Raleigh's half-brother Humphrey Gilbert presented Queen Elizabeth I with 'A discourse of a discouerie for a new passage to Cataia [Cathay] – the onely way for our princes to possesse the wealthe of all the Easte parts of the world'. Sadly, the Queen ignored his proposal and it was ten years before Frobisher managed to persuade the Muscovy Company to license his expedition. Then, with the help of Michael Lok, the Company's director, he was able to raise enough capital. With two barks, *Gabriel* and *Michael*, of about 20–25 tons each, a pinnace or tender of 10 tons and a total crew of 35, he sailed on 7 June 1576.

In command of *Gabriel*, he promptly lost touch with both *Michael* and the smaller vessel in a storm, but pressed on and reached Labrador in July. Prevented by the ice from venturing farther north, he entered the bay which is now named after him and penetrated what he hoped would prove to be a strait leading to 'open sea on the back side'.

Instead he found himself, on 18 August, in a deep bay off the southeastern coast of an island later to be named Baffin. As well as meeting the local Inuit, he found 'sundry kind of Beastes in great plenty as Beares, Dere, Hares, Foxes and Dogges'. Here he collected 'a piece of a black stone' which on return to England he convinced merchants, in spite of sceptical assayers, contained gold.

The next year, for his second voyage, Frobisher was engaged to command an expedition by the newly formed Company of Cathay. Serious additional backing came from the Queen, who provided the 18-gun ship *Ayde* and the then very substantial sum of £1,000 towards expenses. Frobisher was appointed High Admiral of all lands and waters that might be discovered by him. On 27 May 1577 the expedition sailed. With *Ayde* and 15 other vessels, and accompanied by 100 miners and other men including refiners, soldiers and 'gentlemen', he reached his eponymous bay on 17 July, taking formal possession in the Queen's name. Some 1,200 tons of the 'black stone' were successfully brought back to England, but somewhat less successfully transmuted into gold. The Cathay Company went bankrupt. Frobisher had penetrated further north than anyone else at that time, but concluded that he had reached impassable ice. For all that, news of the abundant whales he had seen quickened the fishermen's pulses and ensured an influx of adventurous whalers who would hunt and inevitably chart new waters.

## John Davis and the 'white beares'

In January 1583, John Davis, Gentleman, 'a man very well grounded in the principles of the Arte of Navigation', benefitting from his friendship with fellow explorers Adrian Gilbert – brother to the Humphrey mentioned above – and

Walter Raleigh, had the chance to propose an expedition to one of the Queen's most powerful courtiers, Francis Walsingham. As a result, Davis sailed from Dartmouth in June 1585 with *Sunneshine* (50 tons) and *Mooneshine* (35 tons) on the first of three voyages as 'chief Captaine and Pilot Generall, for the search and discoverie of the north-west passage to China'. Crossing the Denmark Strait to the ice-bound east coast of Greenland, he rounded Cape Farewell and coasted the ice-free waters of western Greenland before heading northwest across what would become the Davis Strait, finding Baffin Island at 66°N and giving us an early report of an encounter with the wildlife there:

> When wee came neere the shore, wee found white
> beares of a monstruous bignesse: we being desirous
> of fresh victual and the sport, began to assault
> them, and I being on land one of them came down
> the hill right against me; my piece was charged with

*Late 16th-century bear encounter.*

haileshot and a bullet, tooke the water straighte, making small account of his hurt. We followed him on our boate, and killed him with boare spears, and two more that night.

He reached well into what would become Cumberland Sound but turned back in August in order to avoid the winter freeze, reporting optimistically to his employers, 'The northwest passage is a matter nothing doubtful, but at anytime almost to be passed' and that the sea was 'voyde of yse and the waters very deepe'.

On his second attempt, in May 1586, in spite of great trouble with the 'marveilous theevish' Inuit, he explored the coast of Labrador. Enduring foul and stormy weather, with men wounded and two killed by Inuit, he again turned back. But he again confirmed news of great value, the abundance of fish and whales.

A year later, Davis sailed on a third and last voyage – in pursuit of both fish and exploration – with the barks *Elizabeth* and *Sunneshine* and the pinnace *Helene*. Now he hugged the western coast of Greenland, avoiding the heavy ice on the Canadian side of the strait, penetrating his furthest north, 72°12', only to be well and truly blocked by ice from discovering the entrance to the Passage (this was at the time of the hard conditions of the Little Ice Age). Nevertheless, on return to Dartmouth, he wrote to his employer William Sanderson, 'I have been in 73 degrees, finding the sea all open, and forty leagues betweene land and land. The passage is most probable, the execution easie.'

Though Davis failed in his primary object, his achievements rank with those of William Baffin and Henry Hudson, seamen who followed in his track. Many Arctic place names commemorate him, not least that of the Davis Strait. Later, John Ross called him 'an enterprising and persevering seaman', which doubtless would have pleased him greatly. Although Davis planned to try for the entrance to the passage 'by the backe partes of America', this came to nothing and he never returned to the Arctic. He did, however, later explore the South Atlantic and discover the Falkland Islands.

## More failures

At the end of the 16th century it was the Dutch who were diligently investigating the possibility of a passage through to the Pacific, but their efforts were directed to the putative Northern Route across the top of Siberia. The great navigator Willem Barents failed to achieve it but, as with those who were penetrating the Davis Strait, he found an abundance of wildlife in the waters of Svalbard. This galvanised the whalers and inevitably improved the Arctic charts, for all that the whaling captains tended to keep their discoveries secret.

Sponsored by the Dutch, Henry Hudson tried and failed to find a way to the Orient by way of the North Pole and the Siberian Arctic. But when he went west in 1610 – in *Discovery*, the first of a series of distinguished ships of that name – to take advantage of John Davis's discoveries, he struck gold, or, more accurately, fur, when he explored the great bay which now bears his name. This was a huge leap

*Hudson's* Discovery.

forward for commerce, but it still hadn't opened the door to the Passage.

In 1616 the Muscovy Company hired Captain Robert Bylot to continue the search for the Northwest Passage (Bylot had been first mate on Hudson's *Discovery*). He was accompanied as pilot by William Baffin, an active seaman, English navigator and explorer who had served the Company for two years in the Spitsbergen whale-fishery as pilot aboard the *Tiger*, flagship of the whaling fleet. Together, Bylot and Baffin sailed high above the Arctic Circle, circumnavigating and charting what was to become Baffin Bay. They reached 77°45'N and discovered Lancaster Sound, without knowing that it held the key to the Passage, not to be transited for another three centuries.

On this voyage Bylot and Baffin sailed nearly 300 nautical miles farther north than John Davis, and for 236 years this farthest north remained unbeaten. They had shown that it was possible to penetrate much further north than anything yet accomplished, but it was their opinion that they had reached a dead end. Back in England their careful work in Baffin Bay was doubted by Admiralty cartographers, whose charts showed the discoveries only as a dotted bulge implying 'unsurveyed'. When the bay was 'rediscovered' by Sir John Ross 200 years later, however, Bylot and Baffin's charts were found to be extremely accurate.

Fifteen years after Bylot and Baffin, the explorer Luke Foxe persuaded London merchants to send him to investigate Hudson Bay. He failed to discover the strait leading west from what became Foxe Basin and concluded that the Passage did not exist. At the same time the Bristol Society of Merchant Venturers, fearing that the Londoners might be looking for a monopoly on Northwest Passage rights, set up their own

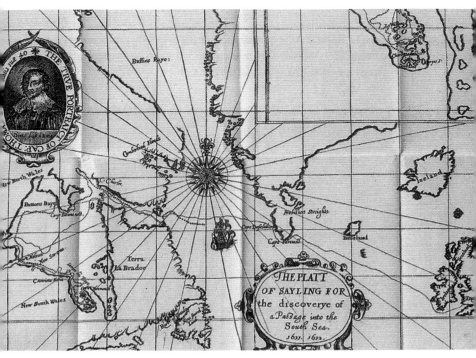

*Captain James' chart: he described his voyage as 'Strange and Dangerous'.*

expedition, led by Captain Thomas James. They petitioned Charles I and won an agreement establishing equal rights in any discoveries for either city. James's 1631 voyage, in *Henrietta Maria* (named after Charles's queen), was eventful in the sense of foul weather and icy encounters: '...we were beset with many extraordinary pieces of ice that came upon us, as it were, with willful violence.'

James was no more successful than Foxe in unravelling the hoped-for Passage. Limping back to Bristol, he wrote a classic account of the misfortunes of *The Strange and Dangerous Voyage*. The search for the Northwest Passage lost momentum. But in 1670 the incorporation of the Hudson's Bay Company led to land-based mapping of the Canadian coasts and a two-pronged attack on the Passage from both east and west.

# THE PACIFIC APPROACH

The Frenchman Jacques Cartier had been first to search for an approach from the Pacific, in three voyages between 1534 and 1541. Two and a half centuries later, he was followed by Captain James Cook, with *Resolution* and *Discovery*, on the last of his three great voyages around the world. In November 1778 Cook went through the strait named after Vitus Bering, a Danish-born navigator in the Russian navy; entering the Chukchi Sea to the northwest, he found his way blocked by impenetrable ice. He turned back, to meet his death in Hawaii.

By this time it had been shown conclusively that there was no navigable route in the temperate latitudes between the Pacific and the Atlantic Oceans. But voyages had added to the sum of geographic knowledge about the Western Hemisphere, particularly of North America. As that knowledge grew, attention gradually turned once again toward the American Arctic.

In 1816, in the service of Russia, Otto von Kotzebue explored the Arctic side of the Bering Strait, searching for

*James Cook, having reached the Chukchi Sea from the Pacific end of the Passage, turns back from the impenetrable ice.*

a Northwest Passage; he named the Kotzebue Sound on the Seward Peninsula. But that was as far as he got. Another 32 years were to pass before Robert McClure in *Investigator* made real advances from the Pacific side.

Geographic exploration had been rudely interrupted by the Napoleonic Wars in the early years of the 19th century. But when Napoleon was exiled to St Helena in 1815 the British Navy was left without an immediate challenge to its supremacy and with a lot of ships and sailors keen to distinguish themselves.

In 1817 William Scoresby, a successful whaling skipper with much understanding of the natural history of Arctic waters, had written to Joseph Banks, President of the Royal Society, proposing further attempts at the Northwest Passage in the light of vastly increased knowledge of polar navigation; he pointed out that from his own experience the current ice conditions were sympathetic. Banks, knowing Scoresby's qualifications, supported the idea. Barrow, when consulted,

## Barrow's patronage

The most significant figure in sponsoring expeditions in search of the Passage during this period was John Barrow, Permanent Secretary to the British Admiralty. With a navy champing at the bit, Barrow found himself in a position to promote voyages of discovery; the Arctic offered rich pickings. Between 1816 and 1845 he posted ships and eager sailors in search of northern science and British glory. At the same time, the Board of Longitude offered £5,000 sterling to the first to cross the 110°W meridian, £10,000 for the 130° and £20,000 for breaking through to the Pacific. Serious prizes.

was enthusiastic, but regrettably chose not to ask the highly competent Scoresby to command an expedition. Instead, in 1818, he sent Captain John Ross and Lieutenant William Edward Parry to search with the whalers *Isabella* (368 tons, 58 crew) and *Alexander* (252 tons, 37 crew).

*Joseph Banks, President of the Royal Society.*

## The mythical mountains

Ross planned to explore the island region discovered and charted by Bylot and Baffin 200 years before. Despite the doubts that had been cast on those earlier charts, Ross found them entirely trustworthy and took pleasure in 'rediscovering' correctly plotted geographic features. Reaching the extreme north of the island, he found the entrance to Lancaster Sound. Without knowing the significance of his find – it would later prove to be the main entrance to the Passage – he turned back, against the strongly expressed disapproval of his officers. He believed that it was a dead end, the way ahead blocked by mountains he named after John Wilson Croker, parliamentarian and Secretary to the Admiralty. In *A Voyage of Discovery*, published the following year, he wrote:

> I distinctly saw the land, round the bottom of the bay, forming a connected chain of mountains with those which extended along the north and south sides… At this moment I also saw a continuity of ice, at the distance of seven miles, extending from one side of the bay to the other…

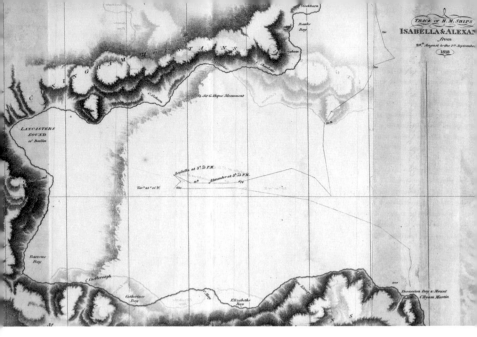

*John Ross's chart of the 'Croker Mountains'.*

It was a decision which caused him real grief, for the mountains did not exist.

## Parry's successes, Ross and 'the man who ate his boots'

Like his fellow officers, Parry was unimpressed at Ross's decision, feeling 'that attempts at Polar discovery had been relinquished just at a time when there was the greatest chance of succeeding'. In the following year, now promoted captain, he returned to the same waters with the bomb *Hecla* ('bombs' were heavily built ships, constructed to deal with the recoil from heavy mortars, which made them particularly suitable for polar work) and Matthew Liddon's gun-brig *Griper*. Parry promptly sailed through the imaginary Croker Mountains, upsetting Captain Ross, and carried on to the west through what became the Parry Channel. He named Beechey Island and its useful harbour after his first lieutenant, Frederick William Beechey, and, becoming the first European to

18

winter in the Canadian Arctic Archipelago at Melville Island, collected his £5,000 prize for crossing the 110°W meridian on 4 September. He was well on the way to proving the existence of a big-ship route to the Pacific.

Now Barrow sent Lieutenant John Franklin to lead an overland expedition from Hudson Bay to chart more of the coast to the east of the Coppermine River.

Between 1819 and 1822 Franklin lost 11 of the 20 men in his party. Most died of starvation, but there was at least one murder and suggestions of cannibalism. The survivors lived on a diet of lichens, even tackling the leather of their boots. Franklin became known as 'the man who ate his boots'.

Parry's second attempt on the Passage, in 1821–3, was as commander of the bomb *Fury*; he was accompanied by George Lyon in *Hecla*. This time he entered Hudson Bay to cross the

Hecla *and* Fury *cutting through the ice to Winter Island, on the southern coast of Melville Peninsula, October 1821.*

Foxe Basin, where he failed to find a way through to the west by a likely looking channel that was blocked by ice – he named it Fury and Hecla Strait. Once again, as when he had sailed with Ross, he confirmed the accuracy of Baffin's tidal and astronomical observations two centuries before.

His last expedition in search of the Passage was in 1824–5, this time back in command of *Hecla*, while Henry Hoppner joined *Fury*. It was a disaster. Having entered Lancaster Sound, they turned down Prince Regent Inlet only for *Fury* to be severely damaged by ice while overwintering on the coast of Somerset Island. In the end her stores were unloaded onto Fury Beach (72°30'N, 91°00'W) in August 1825. They returned home in *Hecla*, abandoning what was left of *Fury* to serve as a victualling yard for many Arctic explorers over the next decades.

In May 1829 John Ross, a somewhat cantankerous individual, still smarting from the Croker Mountains mistake but admitting he 'might have been wrong' and looking for restitution, organised finance for a second, private expedition, bringing the side-wheeler steamship *Victory* to Prince Regent Inlet. Like *Fury*, she came to grief in the ice in what Ross called Felix Harbour, after his benefactor, Felix Booth (of Booth's gin). They were to be beset through four long ice-ridden winters, the summer melt so insignificant that even then they could hardly move. But much useful work occupied their enforced time ashore. With the help of local Inuit they explored the regions to the north and west. In 1831 the captain's nephew James Clark Ross reached and fixed a position for the north magnetic pole, at that time on the Boothia Peninsula. (Because of variations in the earth's magnetic field, the magnetic pole is constantly on the move: today it is closer to Resolute, on the Parry Channel.) Sledge-based parties discovered King William Island, though they wrongly thought it part of the mainland.

After four years, and with the onset of scurvy, they abandoned their ship (by then beset in what they called Victory Harbour) on 28 May 1832, sledging the coast north to the abandoned stores and the remains of *Fury*, left there by Parry seven years earlier. Another year went by before a break in the ice finally allowed them to get away, using *Fury's* longboats. Heading north to Lancaster Sound, by amazing coincidence, they were eventually rescued by the whaler *Isabella*, the vessel which Ross had commanded on his 1818 expedition. He brought home to a hero's welcome 19 of the 22 men he set out with, a record which compared very favourably with previous expeditions. Both Rosses gained knighthoods in an audience with King William IV. James was promoted to captain and went on to immense distinction as an explorer in both polar regions. John regained his reputation and ended with a clutch of gold medals as Admiral Sir John Ross, CB.

*Ross's crew rescued by the whaler* Isabella.

## JOHN FRANKLIN: A DOOMED VOYAGE

Exploration of the Arctic mainland after Franklin's shore-based work had by now left less than 500km of uninvestigated Northwest Territory coast. Barrow decided the time was overdue to complete the charting of the still-putative Northwest Passage. The highly competent James Clark Ross declined an offer to command an expedition – not surprisingly, as he had only just returned from four very successful years in the Antarctic. Franklin, however, despite his age (59), accepted the task. A younger man, James Fitzjames, was given command of *Erebus*; Francis Crozier, who had been in the Antarctic with James Ross, was reappointed to *Terror*. Captain Sir John Franklin, as he now was, received official instructions on 5 May 1845 to proceed from the Davis Strait 'towards Bering Strait in as straight a line as is permitted by ice or any unknown land'. But his last expedition was destined to end in disaster and upset the plans of the Royal Navy for decades.

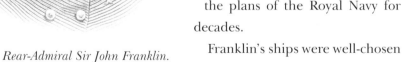

*Rear-Admiral Sir John Franklin.*

Franklin's ships were well-chosen for the job. *Erebus* and *Terror* (both roughly 380 tons) were *Hecla*-class bomb vessels, particularly suitable for the polar work in which they had already proved themselves in the ice of the Antarctic. New-fangled steam engines provided 4 knots independently of sail, plus the delights of plentiful fresh water and heat. Rudder and screw were retractable as protection from the ice. Most of the crew were English, joined by a few Scots and Irishmen; they were to enjoy a library of a thousand books. Galley supplies, from the grandest grocers in London, Fortnum & Mason, were stowed against a possible three years at sea.

The expedition sailed from the London port of Greenhithe on 19 May 1845 with a crew of 24 officers and 110 men. In Greenland's Disko Harbour (Ilulisat today), the oxen carried by the transport ship *Barretto Junior* were slaughtered and the fresh meat transferred to *Erebus* and *Terror*. Crew members wrote their last letters home, revealing that Franklin banned swearing and drunkenness. Five men were discharged 'unfit' and sent home in the transport, reducing the two ships' final crew size to 129.

Erebus *had just returned from a triumphant Antarctic expedition. Refitted and stocked with London's finest groceries, she was ideally suited to an Arctic adventure.*

The expedition sailed for Baffin Bay, where in early August they met the skippers of the whalers *Prince of Wales* and

*Enterprise* and enjoyed the traditional 'gam' – an exchange of news and conversation. This was to be the last the world heard of Franklin and his men for nearly ten years.

## The search begins

John Ross, who had had plenty of experience of Arctic hazards, was the first to become concerned about the lack of news. He urged a search, but two years passed without word before Franklin's wife Jane eventually persuaded the Admiralty to consider the situation. Because the expedition carried supplies

for three years, the Lords Commissioners waited yet another year, till 1848, before offering a £20,000 reward. At this point, of course, no one knew where in the unknown and uncharted region Franklin might be – whether it would be more productive to search from the east or west end. So the first efforts were two-pronged.

From the Atlantic, James Clark Ross in HMS *Enterprise* and Edward Bird in *Investigator* entered Lancaster Sound. They were hampered by heavy ice and, though they searched Somerset Island by sledge, found no trace. From the Pacific and the Bering Strait, Thomas Moore in *Plover* and Henry Kellett in *Herald* entered the Beaufort Sea, also without success. It was not until two years later, in the summer of 1850, that real advances were made.

Richard Collinson, HMS *Enterprise*, accompanied by Commander Robert McClure, *Investigator*, led an expedition to the Pacific, with orders to continue charting the Arctic coast and to search for Franklin. Before they reached the Bering Strait they were separated. *Investigator* got to the north of Banks Island before becoming trapped in the ice of a bay McClure named Mercy Bay. After enduring two winters beset, he sledged east, reaching Melville Island, the position achieved by Parry from the west in 1820; he thus forged the last link of the Passage, showing that the transit by sea was possible in more sympathetic ice conditions. Abandoning his doomed ship on 3 June 1853, McClure sent Samuel Gurney Cresswell on ahead with letters for the Admiralty. Cresswell first sledged to reach *Phoenix* at Beechey Island and got to Britain in 1853, thus becoming the first man, if not ship, to complete a transit of the Passage. The captain and the rest of the complement arrived a year later.

*Cresswell 'sledging over hummocky ice' in April 1853.*

Collinson chose to explore south of Banks Island, wintering in Cambridge Bay. Sledge parties explored the coast of Victoria Island and, without knowing it, were at one time only 60km from the lost Franklin ships. Though Collinson didn't sail it, he too showed that the Passage was possible.

## The first clues

The greater prize, and partial success in searching for Franklin, had been found inside the eastern entrance. Captain Horatio Austin, in command of *Resolute* and *Assistance*, entered Lancaster Sound in 1850. In the summer the party found traces of *Erebus* and *Terror* on the coast of Devon Island, where Captain Erasmus Ommaney of *Assistance* wrote, 'I had the satisfaction of meeting with the first traces of Sir John Franklin's expedition, consisting of fragments of naval stores, ragged portions of clothing, preserved meat tins etc.' Continuing to search the coast of Devon Island, they came to Parry's old anchorage off Beechey Island, where they found the foundations of buildings, cairns and the graves of three crewmen: Royal Marine William Braine and Able Seaman John Hartnell of *Erebus* and Leading Stoker John Torrington of *Terror*. However, to their very great surprise, they found no written record of Franklin's plans nor anything to indicate where he and the ships might have gone. Austin returned home early to a welcome which tended to suggest he might have tried harder. At this time there was still uncertainty as to the whereabouts of Collinson and McClure. Frustration set in.

## The 'Arctic Squadron'

The British Admiralty's last effort in searching for Franklin was an expedition commanded by Captain Sir Edward Belcher, who sailed from the Nore on the Thames Estuary in

*The 1852 'Arctic squadron'.*

April 1852 with an 'Arctic squadron' of five ships – *Resolute*, *Assistance*, *Pioneer*, *Intrepid* and *North Star*. In spite of a good deal of successful surveying by sledge – a triumph of man-hauling, in which several officers pointed out that dog-sledging had much to recommend it – the enterprise suffered greatly from the ice. Francis McClintock, who was searching along the Parry Channel in *Intrepid*, rescued Robert McClure, who had already abandoned *Investigator*. (As the first to prove the Northwest Passage a viable proposition, even though he had not sailed it, McClure shared with his crew a £10,000 prize presented by the Admiralty, comfortably after he had been acquitted at the inevitable court-martial for the loss of his ship.)

The Belcher expedition was a disaster of epic proportions, the members returning home leaving a string of abandoned ships. The Arctic Archipelago was littered with discarded vessels, some wrecks, some sound. *Resolute*, firmly beset but in good shape, was reluctantly abandoned by Captain Henry Kellett in response to firm orders from Belcher, his superior. Freeing herself unaided in the spring thaw, the unmanned vessel, still girdled with ice, drifted through the Parry Channel and found her way out of Lancaster Sound to be boarded a year later by an American whaler's crew in the Davis Strait. In an impressive act of salvage, a scratch crew jury-rigged her and took her to their home port in Connecticut; a generous Congress refitted her and gave her back to a somewhat embarrassed Admiralty. When *Resolute* was subsequently broken up, Queen Victoria presented a splendid desk made of her timber to US President Rutherford Hayes (President Obama still had it in the Oval Office in 2012).

PUNCH, OR THE LONDON CHARIVARI.—December 13, 1856.

THE RETURN OF THE "RESOLUTE."—A GRACEFUL GIFT FROM BROTHER JONATHAN.

*A gift prolonging embarrassment for the Admiralty.*

## John Rae's discovery

What little we know of the fate of the Franklin party came first not from any effort of the Admiralty but from Dr John Rae of the Hudson's Bay Company. Rae was a Scottish explorer highly regarded by the Inuit: impressed after he had covered

*Items from Franklin's expedition bought from the Inuit by John Rae.*

some 1,500km of the coast in little over a month, they called him *Aglooka* – 'he who takes long strides'. Trekking in the spring of 1854, making the third of his overland expeditions in search of Franklin, Rae followed the coast east from the Coppermine River to show first that the Boothia Peninsula was indeed a peninsula and that James Ross's King William Land was in fact King William Island.

Not only did Rae fill in the last gaps in mapping this critical area, but he met Inuit who were able to tell him what had happened to Franklin's lost men. Using sign language, they indicated that earlier in the year they had seen a party of perhaps 40 men dragging a sledge with a boat along the shore of King William Island. The men had lost their ships and were travelling south in search of food. Later the Inuit found the corpses of some 30 men who had succumbed to the cold and starvation. Rae bought a number of items – a gold watch, knives, papers and some silverware marked with initials that proved they were from the Franklin expedition. But what caused a great deal of consternation when his report was leaked to the press in Britain was the suggestion that the corpses showed signs of cannibalism.

## Lady Franklin's Lament

Victorian society was outraged by the suggestion of cannibalism. Rae was condemned to ignominy. Ballads such as 'Lady Franklin's Lament', commemorating the search for her lost husband, became popular.

We were homeward bound one night on the deep
Swinging in my hammock I fell asleep
I dreamed a dream and I thought it true
Concerning Franklin and his gallant crew
With a hundred seamen he sailed away
To the frozen ocean in the month of May
To seek a passage around the pole
Where we poor sailors do sometimes go.
Through cruel hardships they vainly strove
Their ships on mountains of ice were drove
Only the Eskimo with his skin canoe
Was the only one that ever came through
In Baffin's Bay where the whale fish blow
The fate of Franklin no man may know
The fate of Franklin no tongue can tell
Lord Franklin alone with his sailors do dwell
And now my burden it gives me pain
For my long-lost Franklin I would cross the main
Ten thousand pounds I would freely give
To know on earth, that my Franklin do live.

## In the crew's own words

Lady Franklin fought for renewed searches and in fact they continued through much of the rest of the century. But,

*McClintock's* Fox.

crucially, in 1858 she organised a private expedition, led by
Francis McClintock – 'an enterprising and energetic officer'
– with the yacht *Fox*, to search for more news, relics and
records. After wintering in Prince Regent Inlet, McClintock
and Lieutenant William Hobson set off in two sledge parties.
Their Danish interpreter learned from Inuit that two ships
had been beset near King William Island. Like Dr Rae, they
were even able to buy odds and ends of silverware, uniform
buttons and knives. Sledging to the island in early 1859,
they found abandoned boats, relics and three corpses. Most
significantly, they found cairns with message canisters.

The standard Admiralty form, left by Captains Fitzjames
and Crozier and dated 25 April 1848, revealed that *Terror and
Erebus* had been beset in the ice at a position north of King
William Island, 69°52'N 98°39'W, in September 1846. They
had set up camp ashore and wintered in the vicinity of the
island for two years. The form confirmed that Rear-Admiral
Sir John Franklin KCH FRGS RN died of unspecified causes

on 11 June 1847 and that the icebound ships were abandoned on 26 April 1848.

We now know that having entered the labyrinth in Lancaster Sound the Franklin expedition spent the winter of 1845–6 at Beechey Island, then explored the Wellington Channel and rounded Cornwallis Island to enter the Peel Sound towards Victoria Strait. They became beset in the ice north of King William Island, the site of their final encampment. On abandoning their ships, the surviving crew trekked south towards Chantrey Inlet, the Great Fish River (now the Back River) and civilisation, looking for hunting possibilities and food. Nine officers and 15 men had already died; the rest would perish along the way, most on the island and another 30 or 40 on the northern coast of the mainland, hundreds of kilometres from the nearest Western outpost. Not one of the 129 survived.

Between 1847 and 1859 at least 36 expeditions, by both land and sea, were involved in the search. More ships and men were lost looking for Franklin than in the expedition itself. But the Franklin name is well remembered. And the name of Sir John Barrow, 1st Baronet FRS, FRGS (1764–1848) is also commemorated in the Barrow Strait, Point Barrow and the city of Barrow in Alaska. Ross, Parry and Franklin himself all owed him a great deal.

The fate of the two ships and their men has always been the subject of much speculation and active research. In 1997, more than 140 years after Dr Rae's report, marks cut by a blade were identified on the bones of some of the skeletons found on King William Island, vindicating Rae's account of cannibalism. In the mid-1980s, Owen Beattie, Professor of Anthropology from the University of Alberta, began a series of studies of the graves and other physical evidence left on

## Toxic provisions?

The earlier assumption that lead from the poorly sealed cans of meat had been a prime cause of the ill health of Franklin's crew was challenged by a research paper published in 2008, which cast suspicion on the freshwater lead-pipe plumbing system on the ships, a system which was unique to the Franklin expedition. The bodies of Franklin's officers and men carried very high levels of lead, while the crews of other vessels in the navy, supplied at the same time with the same tinned provisions, remained relatively unaffected.

Beechey Island. He examined the three bodies, finding them to be remarkably well preserved. He concluded that the men had most likely died of pneumonia and perhaps tuberculosis. Doubtless the old maritime curse, scurvy, contributed to the tragedy too. Toxicological reports also allowed for the long-suspected lead poisoning as a factor.

### The fate of the crew

In 2009 Robert Grenier, a Senior Marine Archaeologist at Parks Canada, examined sheet metal and copper recovered from 19th-century Inuit hunting sites. He suggested that these samples had once belonged to the *Terror* and formed part of her antifouling protection. After studying Inuit oral testimony, including eyewitness descriptions of starving, exhausted men staggering through the snow without thinking to ask local people how they survived in such a wilderness, Grenier concluded that contemporary official accounts – that all the surviving expedition members abandoned their ice-locked ships – were incorrect. He believes that both ships drifted south, with at least two caretaker crew on board. Inuit hunters arriving at their summer hunting grounds reported discovering one of them adrift in a cove. (European vessels were, of course, a source of much wonder to the Inuit; they represented a treasure trove of timber, copper and iron tools.)

The ship was said to be found in neat and orderly condition, properly shipshape, but when the hunters ventured below with their seal-oil lamps they found a tall dead man in an inner cabin. They also reported that one of the masts was on fire. Grenier wonders if what they saw was the galley chimney still smoking from a meal cooked that morning, before the shore-going party abandoned the vessel. He concluded that the combined evidence of all studies suggested that lead poisoning and disease, including scurvy, along with general exposure to a hostile environment without adequate clothing and nutrition, had led to hypothermia and starvation. Whatever the cause, the result was that everyone on the

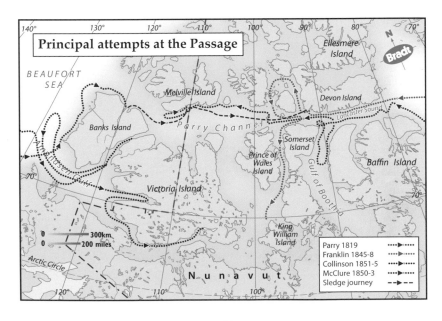

expedition died in the three years following its last sighting
by Europeans in Greenland in 1845.

## Search for the wrecks

Franklin's ships, or what remains of them, wherever they are,
are now in the care of the Government of Canada, which
has designated them a National Historic Site. In 2008 Parks
Canada and its Underwater Archaeological Service started
a three-year series of projects working from the Coastguard
icebreaker *Sir Wilfrid Laurier*. Taking full advantage of Inuit
oral history, it aimed at finding *Erebus* and *Terror*, working on
the assumption that they might be on the bottom of Victoria
Strait or Queen Maud Gulf. (In 2010 the remains of McClure's
*Investigator* were discovered in Mercy Bay, Banks Island, by
archaeologists of Parks Canada; the ship was upright and well
preserved, in 8m of water.)

All in all, it was a long time before the whole of the sad
story of Franklin's exhibition was revealed, but it played a
major part in finally charting Canada's northern archipelago.

*Canadian coastguard icebreakers search for
the remains of Franklin's ships.*

## AMUNDSEN: SUCCESS AT LAST

And still explorations went on. The Finnish-Swedish geologist and explorer Adolf Nordenskjöld took *Vega* through the Northeast Passage in 1878–9, but it was not until 45 years after the Franklin searches were largely abandoned that the Northwest Passage was first navigated, by the Norwegian Roald Engelbregt Gravning Amundsen.

Amundsen was born in 1872 to a family of ship-owners. His mother wanted to keep him out of shipping and pressurised him to become a doctor. However, after she died (when he was 21), he abandoned his studies and made his first voyage to a polar region as part of the Belgian Antarctic Expedition of 1897–9: he served as mate to Adrien de Gerlache, in command of *Belgica*, when he led the first party to winter south of the Antarctic Circle. Inspired by the exploits of his countryman, Fridtjof Nansen, Amundsen then planned to conquer the Northwest Passage in pursuit of Norwegian glory.

*Gjøa* (pronounced 'Joe'), a 70-foot 48-ton fishing sloop, had been built in 1872 and endured a life of herring fishing and hard knocks before Amundsen bought her in 1900. Although she was decidedly smaller than conventional Arctic vessels, his

*Amundsen's sloop* Gjøa.

theory was that her shallow draft would make it easier for her to negotiate the inevitable shoals and the small crew would to a large extent be able to live off the land. She was also all he could afford.

After a shake-down sealing cruise in the Barents Sea, Amundsen set about giving *Gjøa* a much-needed refit. He strengthened frames and planking and installed a 13-horsepower single-screw Dan hot-bulb petrol engine. In the spring of 1902 he looked for sponsors for his proposed expedition, cannily persuading King Oscar to support him. This was at a time when Norwegian nationalism was increasing and the union of the kingdoms of Norway and Sweden, which had been jointly ruled by a Swedish monarch for nearly a century, was easing towards dissolution.

As expedition leader, Amundsen assembled a powerful crew. Godfred Hansen, a Danish naval lieutenant, became *Gjøa's* chief officer and Helmer Hanssen, an experienced ice pilot, second officer. The rest of the complement consisted of Anton Lund, an experienced sealing captain; Peder Ristvedt, engineer; Gustav Juel Wiik, second engineer; and Adolf Henrik Lindstrøm, cook.

## Completing the Passage

*Gjøa* sailed from the Oslo fjord on 16 June 1903 and made for Baffin Bay. Entering by way of Lancaster and Peel Sounds and James Ross Strait, she came to King William Island, where Amundsen and his men spent two winters in a snug harbour they called Gjøa Haven. One more winter was spent off King Point in Mackenzie Bay before they finally broke free to sail on towards the Beaufort Sea.

Amundsen passed along the Yukon coast in the summer of 1905, though *Gjøa* was held up again and had to winter in the ice just short of Herschel Island. But as first to sail it from end to end he had conquered the Northwest Passage. Leaving his crew on board, he set off to ski 800km to the tiny settlement of Eagle, on the Alaskan side of the border, in order to telegraph

*Amundsen wrote to* The Times.

the news ($700 collect! – he had no money) to Nansen for forwarding to *The Times* in London, fulfilling a contract promising a fat fee. However, skulduggery intervened.

The message was passed to newspapers in Seattle. *The Times* was denied a scoop. Nansen refused to pay the bill. Amundsen, knowing nothing of this betrayal, returned to *Gjøa*. She remained icebound until 11 July, when they sailed on towards the Bering Sea and civilisation.

Amundsen and his crew completed the three-year passage by arriving at Nome, Alaska, on 31 August 1906, to become the first to navigate the icy labyrinth of the Arctic Archipelago, achieving something that had frustrated explorers for more than 400 years.

Now he heard that Norway had formally become independent of Sweden. He promptly sent the newly crowned King Haakon VII news of his success, feeling that it 'was a great achievement for Norway'. He said he hoped to do more and signed himself 'Your loyal subject, Roald Amundsen'. He then sailed on to earthquake-ravaged San Francisco, where the expedition was met with a hero's welcome on 19 October. By the time he returned home he and his crew had become the new country's first national heroes. And he went on to become a key expedition leader in the Heroic Age of polar exploration. *Gjøa* was fêted in San Francisco but eventually returned to Oslo in 1972 for a refit and finally, in 2012, a new undercover berth in the extended Fram Museum on the Bygdøy Peninsula.

# AFTER AMUNDSEN

It was to be 34 years before the Passage was again transited by sea, but in 1921 the Danish-Inuit explorer and ethnologist Knud Rasmussen enjoyed the first crossing by dog sledge – the longest such journey recorded at that time. In the company of two Greenlandic hunters, Rasmussen ('Give me winter, give me dogs and you can keep the rest') sledded for 16 months, from Pond Inlet to Nome. In fact he wanted to carry on across the frozen Bering Strait to Russia, but was refused a visa.

In 1940 the first boat since *Gjøa* to transit the Passage was the Royal Canadian Mounted Police's 29.7-metre auxiliary schooner *St Roch*. Under the command of Sergeant Henry Asbjørn Larsen the voyage took 28 months and involved two winters; in 1943 Larsen made the return in one season (*St Roch* may still be seen, in the Vancouver Maritime Museum). In 1954 the icebreaker HMCS *Labrador* carried out the first single-voyage circumnavigation of North America to find a place in the record books.

In 1957 three US coastguard vessels, *Storis*, *Bramble* and *Spar*, surveyed and charted the first deep-water route in the

*The schooner* St Roch.

## Canada's sovereignty claims

One of the objects of the expeditions of the 1940s and '50s had been to confirm Canadian sovereignty over the Passage, in order to forestall any suggestion that it might represent an international highway. In legal terms, sovereignty involves 'effective occupation'. In practice, and leaving aside the use of brute force, this means permanent habitation, policing the boundaries, raising a flag, operating a post office, conducting a census, surveying the natural resources and patrolling. Canada has long concerned itself with these requirements. In 1903 the North West Mounted Police raised the Canadian flag at Herschel Island. Since becoming the Royal Canadian Mounted Police they have penetrated high latitudes well beyond even the areas occupied by the native Inuit in Pond Inlet to include Ellesmere Island.

Parry Channel and in 1969 the ice-strengthened supertanker SS *Manhattan*, modified with an icebreaker bow, broke through, escorted by the Canadian icebreaker *John A Macdonald*, and returned carrying the token cargo of a single barrel of crude oil from Prudhoe Bay. This was the first commercial vessel of economic size to transit the Canadian Arctic Archipelago. Future prospects for freight are difficult to predict, since the Passage is open to heavy traffic for only a couple of months each year and there is little in the way of infrastructure to support it.

*Manhattan's* achievement mainly succeeded in encouraging the construction of the overland TransAlaska Pipeline and prompting vigorous debate in Canada on the sovereignty implications.

In August 1960 USS *Seadragon*, a Skate-class submarine commanded by Lieutenant Commander George P Steele, completed the first underwater transit, entering Lancaster Sound and proceeding through the Parry Channel (using Edward Parry's 1819 journal as a guide!) to exit by the McClure Strait to the Beaufort Sea. By 21 August *Seadragon* was heading for the North Pole and yet again proving that a route over the top of the world was not possible for conventional vessels. For many years it had been assumed that a passage across the North Pole was practical. Many expeditions, including one commanded by Franklin, had worked on the assumption that sea water was incapable of freezing (as late as the mid-18th century, Captain James Cook reported that Antarctic icebergs had yielded fresh water, seemingly confirming the hypothesis).

## The tourist trail

The first expedition passenger vessel transited the Northwest Passage in August 1984 when Captain Hasse Nilsson succeeded with the *Lindblad Explorer* (ice-strengthened class

*In 1984 Lars-Eric Lindblad's* Lindblad Explorer *became the first tourist vessel to complete the Northwest Passage.*

*Hapag-Lloyd's* Hanseatic *has traversed the Passage many times since 1994.*

Germanischer Lloyd DNV ICE-1A). Arriving in Yokohama, she became the first vessel in five centuries to complete a voyage from the Atlantic to the Orient by way of the Passage. Since then, expedition icebreakers and ice-strengthened vessels have made the voyage occasionally during the August/ September open season. In recent years regular transits have been made by the vessels of Hapag-Lloyd, Quark Expeditions, One Ocean Expeditions and Adventure Canada.

Private expedition yachts have become increasingly regular visitors to the archipelago, several large motor yachts making transits with specialist support from EYOS Expeditions. The private residential vessel *The World* will attempt the transit in August 2012, when she could become the largest passenger vessel to succeed.

Bob Headland of the Scott Polar Research Institute calculates that by the end of 2011 the Northwest Passage had been successfully transited 160 times. The journey can be completed in eight days, but most expeditions do it more slowly, taking time to enjoy the abundant wildlife. No one knows how many have tried and failed.

# THE PASSAGE TODAY

Approaching land from Baffin Bay there are two classic entrances, north or south of Bylot Island, which was named by Baffin in honour of his captain after the expedition of 1616. (Doubtless whalers already knew the area, but whalers were always reluctant to publicise their discoveries.) The most convenient plan for any vessel is to enter south of the island, visiting Pond Inlet, where, if you arrange them in advance, there are facilities for customs clearance. There are no official marine ports of entry into Canada north of 60°. The Canadian Federal Government's rules require any vessels of more than 300 gross tons proposing to transit the Passage to report to the Northern Canada Vessel Traffic Services Zone (NORDREG), the registration system maintained by the coast guard.

Whichever choice of approach is made, landfall brings Nunavut.

## NUNAVUT

One of the remotest and most sparsely settled communities in the world, Nunavut became a Territory (with the same powers and responsibilities as the Northwest Territories and

*Nunavut's population of just over 33,000 is spread over an area the size of Western Europe.*

the Yukon – something less than a Province) following the first major change to Canada's map since the incorporation in 1949 of the new province of Newfoundland. Separated officially from the Northwest Territories in 1999, Nunavut – 'our land' – covers most of the Canadian Arctic Archipelago, making it the fifth-largest territorial subdivision in the world. Its estimated population of a bit more than 33,000, mostly Inuit, is spread over an area the size of Western Europe.

*Inuit* means 'the people'; the singular form is *Inuk* or 'person'. *Eskimo* is largely outdated and politically incorrect in Canada, but still appears in the titles of organisations formed when the word was accepted. In Nunavut the native language is Inuktitut, in the Canadian Northwest Territories it is Inuvialut. Across the border in Alaska the native Yupik choose not to accept the word Inuit, preferring Yupik or Eskimo.

Today's Inuit are descended from a Paleo-Eskimo people who crossed the Bering land bridge from Siberia, arriving from Chukotka by way of Alaska perhaps 12,000 years ago. In time these ancient people became the Dorsets, seal and caribou hunters who colonised Nunavut more than 2,000 years ago. They in turn were succeeded some 500 years ago by the Thule, ancestors of the modern Inuit. The Thule culture, noted for its sophisticated tools, built food caches and stone houses, lasted in the area till the 18th-century arrival of the Norse.

Like their predecessors, the modern Inuit made use of caches, hunted caribou and fished for char. They also hunted seals from the ice in winter. Superbly adapted to the rigours of life in a hostile environment, all these colonisers came to Arctic North America as hunter-gatherers. Their tools were made from bones, their clothing – the key to survival – from bird skins and mammal hides, sinew and gut. As land-based hunters they used sleds hauled by huskies – domesticated wolves. Huskies were pack animals and hunting companions, adept at sniffing out seal pups hidden by snow. They also served as guards, warning of polar bears.

In summer, hunters worked at sea, fishing and spearing seals and whales, using one-man *qajaqs* – kayaks, lightly framed of wood and covered with sealskin, capable of being righted even if swamped and overturned. *Umiaks* were larger vessels, 6–12m long, driftwood- or whalebone-framed and covered with walrus or bearded seal skins. Their shallow draft made

*Narwhal-hunting from a kayak.*

them convenient for beaching. They were capable of carrying freight and of moving people and possessions to seasonal hunting grounds; they were also used in hunting walrus and whales. The Inuit diet was low in carbohydrate, high in protein and even higher in fat. It was almost sugar-free: heart problems are still rare among the Inuit. They enjoyed plant material and berries when they were available. Necessary vitamins were no problem even in winter – their vitamin C came from raw seal liver and *muktuk* (whale skin and blubber).

*In Nunavut, quad bikes are perfect for summer hunting and family transport.*

## A few useful expressions
... and be thankful that most Inuit have good English.

| English | Inuktitut |
|---|---|
| Hello | Asuujutit |
| Goodbye | Aingai |
| Thank you | Qujannamiik |
| You're welcome | Ilaali |
| Yes | Ing |
| No | Aagga |
| What is your name? | Kinauvit |
| My name is | Uvanga |
| How are you? | Qanuippit |
| Money | Kiinaujaq |
| When? | Qanga |
| Where? | Nami |
| I feel sick | Qanimmaliqpunga |

Much has changed. The Moravian missionaries, who brought Christianity and the bible in the late 18th century, also developed a written language – Qaliujaaqpait – based on syllabic script. Many of the communities now have broadband internet access. There is even a computer font, Piqiarniq, to say nothing of skidoos and outboard motors.

Nunavut enjoys the highest birth rate in Canada – it is a youthful Territory with an average age of 23. The population is 85% Inuit and it is the Inuit themselves who are largely running the administration. The head of government, the Premier of Nunavut, is elected by the members of a legislative assembly, based in the capital, Iqaluit (Frobisher Bay). Nunavut also elects a single member to the Canadian Parliament. The Territory relies on an annual budget of CAD700 million, provided almost entirely by the Federal Government.

# POND INLET TO BELLOT STRAIT

*Lancaster Sound, Devon Island, Beechey Island, Prince Regent Inlet, Fort Ross, Bellot Strait. This stretch of the Passage offers the best chance of icebergs.*

## Pond Inlet 72°41'N  077°57'W

**Mittimatalik** *'the place where Mitima is buried'*

Captain John Ross arrived here in 1818 in the whaler *Isabella*, naming the anchorage after John Pond, an English astronomer. As of the 2006 census the population of Pond Inlet was 1,315, making it the largest of the four hamlets above the 72nd parallel. Its economy is mainly based on serving the surrounding area, with Government as the largest employer. In January to March average temperatures hover around –25°C, although recent winters have tended to be warmer and drier. But in summer, with an average 7–10°C, the sun shines up to 21 hours a day. Blizzards and high winds

## A note on names

Not surprisingly, the Inuit who were already here had their own name for this and other settlements. So there is something of a problem. It is a characteristic of the Canadian Arctic that some places have become accustomed to their English names and some have retained the original Inuit name in common use. And while Mittimatalik is an Inuit name, and it represents a predominantly Inuit community, the fact is that everyone nowadays, including the locals, calls it Pond Inlet. So the general rule in this book is to use the names which are in common usage by Inuit, incomers and visitors alike, but to give the alternatives where these exist.

*Pond Inlet, the Passage's entry port.*

regularly stall travellers for an extra night or two – something Northerners refer to as being 'weathered-in'. In summer the Arctic high-pressure system sits over the region, resulting in periods of calm or winds that are generally light to moderate with only the occasional gale-force blow. In August and early September, the period of most marine traffic, the weather in Nunavut is fairly stable with light northerly winds

As a tourist destination, Pond Inlet is considered one of Canada's 'jewels of the North' – a picturesque community, surrounded by mountains with spectacular glaciers. Above all, it has a prime position at the beginning of the maze of waterways and islands where there are caribou, ringed seals, narwhals, belugas and polar bears. As with most Inuit settlements, there will be ravens in town, as well as Lapland and snow buntings.

If in need of Arctic gear in Pond Inlet, make for the Co-op, which offers parkas, winter boots, mittens, hats and scarves. Here, also, is one of the few opportunities to buy a narwhal's

## Snow bunting

*Male in summer plumage.*

Also known as snowflakes or Arctic sparrows, snow buntings *Plectrophenax nivalis* are the most abundant songbirds in these high latitudes. Even their legs are insulated with feathers. Apart from the raven, no other passerine can winter so far north. The breeding male is unmistakable, with all-white plumage and a black back, while the female is grey-black.

Snow buntings are busy creatures, hunting insects and seeds over the tundra, boggy marsh, pools and sandy shores. Seeds are their main food and they find an easy living around settlements. Males are first to arrive at the breeding area, appearing in the late spring, when they take and hold individual territories. They sing their courtship song from the eminence of a boulder or hummock, sometimes from high in the sky like a skylark. Successfully paired, they choose a nest-crevice, building a secret nest of grasses, moss and lichens, lined with hair and feathers. The male guards the property while up to six eggs are incubated for a fortnight. The young are cared for by both parents until they fledge and fly before they are ten days old.

In winter, snow buntings stay in the north, forming mobile flocks, at the mercy of a wandering gyrfalcon.

tusk (export licences are strictly controlled and the tusks are marketed with tags proving that they were shot under licence). Explore the town, maybe see a cultural presentation at the Nattinnak Centre.

Pond Inlet is home to the Interpretive Centre of the Sirmilik

*Singing in traditional dress.*

National Park, one of Canada's newest national parks. Named after a majestic glacier north of the community on Bylot Island, it includes a spectacular area of rugged mountains, ice fields and glaciers, coastal lowlands and seabird colonies. Extensive archaeological exploration of the park area revealed that it had been inhabited for thousands of years by predecessors of the modern-day Inuit – always masters of a frugal economy.

**Navy Board Inlet** – heading north, along the west coast of Bylot Island – leads to Lancaster Sound, where **Admiralty Inlet** will be found further to the east along the Baffin Island north shore. The hamlet of Arctic Bay is located on Adams Sound, further south within the inlet.

## Arctic Bay 73°02'N  085°10'W
### Ikpiarjuk *'the pocket'*
In 1872, whaling skipper Willie Adams found the bay and, in commemorating the 'discovery', gave it the name of his vessel, *Arctic*. But, like Pond Inlet, Arctic Bay had been occupied for thousands of years by Inuit who had given it an Inuktitut name. High hills surround the almost landlocked bay, which has the

*The Sirmilik National Park is named after this majestic glacier.*

smallest tidal range in Canada. To the southeast, the flat-topped King George V Mountain dominates the landscape. Once a year, vessels of the Northern Transportation Company deliver supplies to the community. The area is popular with sport hunters who come in search of polar bears, although this must surely change with the listing of the polar bear as a threatened species. Arctic Bay is host to a Midnight Sun Marathon, one of the northernmost contests held in the world.

A road connects Arctic Bay to Nanisivik, *'the place where people find things'*. This was originally a company town built in 1975 to support the lead-zinc mining and mineral-processing operations for the Nanisivik Mine, in production from 1976 to 2002. Since its closure, reclamation to reinstate the tundra landscape has started and the mine's associated port and dock have served as a training site for the Royal Canadian Navy. There are said to be plans for a $60-million deep-water upgrade.

Admiralty Inlet leads to Lancaster Sound, where we find ourselves in the **Parry Channel**, the main big-ship route through the Passage.

## Lancaster Sound

Ships tend to stay on the north side of the Sound, hugging Devon Island, taking advantage of a favourable current and avoiding ice.

**Devon Island** boasts great coastal scenery and a massive ice cap that feeds spectacular glaciers. Sheltered bays offer

## Arctic hare

The Arctic hare *Lepus arcticus* is a truly Arctic animal, found on the barren grounds north of the treeline, all the way from Baffin Island to Herschel. Sometimes known as jackrabbits, these are large hares, weighing up to 5.5kg. They have the short ears typical of Arctic animals,

*Baffin hares are white even in the summer.*

making them less susceptible to cold. Powerful sharp claws and projecting teeth help them to dig for food under the snow in hard conditions. They enjoy the bark and leaves of willow.

Their pelage is grey-brown in summer, moulting to snow-white in winter. But, astonishingly, those at the Baffin end of the range stay winter-white all year round, making them highly visible and, surely, even more attractive to foxes. They are active and sociable creatures, moderately indifferent to contact with people. If you are really lucky, you might see one hop like a kangaroo, forepaws held in the begging position.

The Inuit take them unenthusiastically for the pot but use the skins for clothing.

landings for beach and tundra with good wildlife opportunities. Arctic hares are common here; surprisingly they will be in their white pelage at any time of the year. Belugas may pass by close to the shore.

## Dundas Harbour 74°31'N 082°30'W
**Talluruti** *'a woman's chin with tattoos on it'*

This is an abandoned settlement with an old Royal Canadian Mounted Police camp and several archaeological sites. The RCMP outpost was established in 1924 as part of a Government presence intended to monitor foreign whaling and other activity. The Hudson's Bay Company leased it in 1933. The following year, 52 Inuit were relocated from Cape Dorset, on the south of Baffin Island, doubtless as part of the Canadian Government's efforts to establish sovereignty over the area. The Inuit must have found life even harder than on Baffin Island, as they returned there only 13 years later. The harbour was populated again in the late 1940s to maintain a patrol presence, but closed in 1951 because of ice difficulties.

*The former home of a Thule family, ancestors of the present-day Inuit.*

# Musk ox

Musk oxen *Ovibos moschatus* move ponderously over the tundra on which they graze. A broad flat boss covers the forehead in buffalo style, and the horns sweep down, out and up to sharp tips. Tough and heavily built, they are protected from winter cold down to −50°C by a dense undercoat of woolly fur, topped by outer guard hairs which provide a skirt reaching almost to the ground. The Inuit call the inner fleece *qiviut*. Finest of all wool, it can be knitted to make fabrics of exceptional warmth while remaining very light in weight.

In summer, the oxen feed enthusiastically on the vegetation of the coastal tundra, mainly the twigs of dwarf willow, in order to build up a thick layer of fat. In the rut of high summer, the bulls produce the musk which gives the species its name. This serves as a territorial marker and plays its part in royal battles. The herd of a dozen or so is under the control of a dominant bull. Their only serious predator, apart from man, is the wolf. Under attack, they gather in a tight circle, enclosing the calves and lowering their heads to offer a ring of sharp horns to the circling wolves: an effective defence strategy, except against guns. Some of the healthy Canadian population of musk oxen has been sent to Alaska and Scandinavia to repopulate regions where they had become extinct.

The RCMP detachment was moved to Craig Harbour on Ellesmere Island.

Only the ruins of a few buildings remain, along with the most northern cemetery in Canada. There is a tundra lake with red-throated divers – Qarsauq – and an impressive Thule site. And there is always the chance of a musk-ox herd. Approach with great care; these animals are dangerous as well as shy, charging furiously when disturbed and therefore demanding respect.

Croker Bay is immediately to the west.

## Black-legged kittiwake

This ocean-going gull *Rissa tridactyla* is one of the most numerous of seabirds. It has a slender lemony-yellow bill, short black legs and a demure black eye, giving it a less loutish appearance than most gulls. Flight is buoyant and bounding, with a shallow wing beat. Unlike other gulls, there are no white tips to the wings, which have 'dipped in ink' ends. The call is a pleasantly onomatopoeic *kitty-waa-ake*.

In the breeding season the kittiwakes' habitat extends as far north as there is open water for fishing. They are the only gulls that are exclusively cliff-face nesters: they will even occupy glacier ledges or the face of a snowbank if there are no ice-free ledges. On more conventional cliffs they often share with murres (guillemots). They build cantilevered nests, sometimes on the narrowest ledges of very steep sea-cliffs and caves, places which offer maximum protection from marauding foxes. Typically they cluster in large numbers near the snouts of glaciers, where a constant run-off of fresh water collides with the slightly warmer sea. When great chunks of ice calve, clouds

## Croker Bay 74°41'N 083°15'W

Lying off the southern coast of Devon Island, Croker Bay was named by William Edward Parry in honour of John Wilson Croker, parliamentarian and Secretary to the Admiralty. The 40km-long, deep-water bay is surrounded by terraced mountains which terminate in two very beautiful blue-ice tidewater glaciers – a great place for a thrilling zodiac ride, safely away from the glacier snout. Black-legged kittiwakes patrol, hoping for a calving in the ice to bring plankton animals to the surface.

of kittiwakes gather at the disturbed water to pick off the tiny crustaceans *Thyannoessa inermis* which crowd the surface. They also enjoy communal flights to a freshwater pond to bathe.

The parents feed their young by regurgitation, an adaptation to the confined space in which they live. Newborn chicks are programmed to sit tight, for if they were to walk about they would be in danger of falling to a certain death. The birds defecate carefully over the edge of the nest; there are conspicuous nitrogen-rich patches of white below, encouraging a healthy growth of scurvy-grass. They winter far out at sea.

It was here in 1818 that John Ross, in the whaler *Isabella*, 'rediscovered' sites first explored by Baffin 200 years earlier. His expedition ended when he turned back after charting what he believed were mountains blocking the end of Lancaster Sound. His 'Croker Mountains' proved somewhat insubstantial when Parry sailed through them in *Hecla* the following year.

## Radstock Bay 74°40'N 091°00'W

Like the other landing places off the southern side of Devon Island, this one is accessible from about mid-July to September. A striking landmark is Caswell Tower, a prominence of sedimentary rock rising from the sea; at its base a broad cobblestone beach offers easy access for a zodiac. As with the other landings hereabouts, make sure there are no polar bears. This area is prime den habitat and a summer migratory route for bears heading towards Wellington Channel to the west. Armed bear-patrol sentries are extremely important.

Behind a series of raised beaches in Radstock Bay, scattered whale bones betray early settlement. There are the remains of several Thule houses, partly subterranean dwellings that may have housed as many as several dozen people. The entrances reveal remains of wells and, in some cases, a stone slab for a lintel. There are raised sleeping platforms inside. The roofs were supported by the ribs and jaws of bowhead whales. The settlement was abandoned, probably some 500 to 600 years ago.

Birds may not be particularly abundant, but there should be kittiwakes and fulmars, maybe snow geese and loons. Cape Liddon, on the western headland, has significant populations of black guillemot. You might catch a glimpse of Arctic hare (in this area, as on Devon Island, they will be in their white

*Whale bones framed an ancient dwelling.*

winter pelage even in summer). There may be beluga whales cruising the shoreline. One of Canada's most famous polar-bear research camps is established here – a small hut on top of the cliff.

## Beechey Island 74°71'N 091°85'W

Connected by a causeway to Devon Island and not very large, this is a high-sided pile of sedimentary layers rising from a series of terraced beaches of limestone shale fragments. It is only truly a separate entity at high water, but it offers one of the most rewarding landings on the transit because of its historical significance.

The first European to visit the island, in 1819, was Lieutenant William Edward Parry with HMS *Hecla*. He named it after Frederick William Beechey, his fellow officer, who had distinguished himself the previous year while serving under Franklin on an abortive North Pole expedition.

In 1845 Sir John Franklin chose this protected harbour – Erebus and Terror Bay – for his first winter encampment. It

## Polar bear

The polar bear *Ursus maritimus*, Nanuk, is a huge animal, especially threatening when it stands 3.5m high on its hind legs. A curiously small triangular head sits on top of a long neck and a massive body encased in a thick layer of blubber. It has a roman nose, small eyes and short, round, furry ears. Its long legs are covered with dense fur and its large feet have fine hair even to the toes; the soles are densely hairy. The white fur becomes yellow with age. The long guard hairs form a watertight outer coat over a soft and fluffy undercoat which traps a layer of air against the skin; this allows the bear to swim well without getting soaked through. Once out of the water a quick shake leaves the outer coat almost dry. The guard hairs are air-filled and exceptionally strong. If you find a tuft of white hairs on the shore, try pulling one apart. If it breaks, it belongs to a caribou!

Polar bears are solitary by nature, living perhaps the loneliest life on the planet. The only time both sexes meet is during the spring courtship, but after copulation the male takes no further part in family life. One, sometimes two, helplessly weak cubs are born in a snow den in late December. They are blind and almost naked, but their diet of rich milk – 30% fat – means that by the time the mother breaks free of the den in April the cubs have increased from a birth weight of 700g to a healthy 11kg. At this time, conveniently, ringed seals have just given birth and the new pups are at their most abundant and vulnerable. The mother bear will take care of the cub or cubs, teaching them their predatory trade for a good two years before abandoning them to make their own way over the ice and the polar seas.

Summer is the lean time for polar bears. Deprived of the fast ice with its breeding population of seals, they come ashore to

*Polar bears may live
the loneliest life of any
mammal on the planet.*

snooze the time away on tundra meadows, eating eider ducks and chicks, grazing the sparse vegetation and searching for ripe berries. At this time they are hungry and dangerous and it is inadvisable to wander alone along coastal beaches and tundra. A bear will not often attack, but you should work on the assumption that it is thinking about it. A dropped handkerchief, in the style of a Victorian girl in search of love, may serve to distract it, and flares may discourage it, but take the danger seriously and avoid contact. People do get eaten.

The polar bear population is in decline: strict laws protect them and hunting is tightly controlled. It is prohibited to lure, pursue or otherwise seek out polar bears in such a way as to disturb them or expose either bears or humans to danger. In addition to deterrents which go bang, shore excursions need to be accompanied by a competent guard, armed with large-calibre (.308, 30-06 etc.) hunting rifles or shotguns firing 12-gauge rifled slugs – used only as a last resort. The Canadian Firearms Act requires firearms and handlers be certified and registered.

was here that his ill-fated expedition (see page 22) spent its last 'comfortable' winter before disappearing into the icy vastness. The three graves that Horatio Austin discovered are today marked by replica boards, while the originals are preserved in the Prince of Wales Museum in Yellowknife. (There is a fourth grave, also marked by a replica headboard, in memory of Able Seaman Thomas Morgan of the *Investigator*, who died on 22 May 1854.)

A kilometre or two from the grave site is what remains of Northumberland House, built on the raised beach in 1852–3 by Commander W J S Pullen, *North Star*, of the Belcher expedition. Stone walls, partial wooden structures, coal, barrel staves and a lonely spar mark the site.

The Franklin memorial, a cenotaph, is well-maintained, although time has taken its toll and polar bear claw marks form deep grooves in the hard wood. It carries a plaque in

*The Franklin memorial, a scratching post for polar bears.*

memory of Lieutenant de Vaisseau Joseph René Bellot of the French navy. Bellot was a distinguished explorer who hardened himself for the Arctic winters by sleeping on bare boards with only a thin mattress and one blanket. When he met his first Inuit he endeared himself to them by constructing an artificial leg (his father was a farrier) for a man who was disabled. He drowned on 18 August 1853, slipping and disappearing between ice floes in the nearby Wellington Channel while he was sledging with despatches destined for Captain Belcher. Less

*Northumberland House, memorial in the background.*

impressively, there are some modern memorials which are perhaps not such fitting neighbours alongside those of more than a century and a half ago. Beechey Island was declared a National Historic Site by the Canadian Government in 1979.

West of Beechey Island brings you to the Barrow Strait and the famous **Parry Channel**, which connects Baffin Bay to the Beaufort Sea by the most direct route, but involving serious ice. It is the only practicable big-ship way through the Passage, transited only in favourable conditions and by vessels of icebreaker class. Ships tend to stay on the north side, taking advantage of a favourable current and aiming to avoid as much ice as possible.

In Resolute Bay, named after the Franklin episode's HMS *Resolute*, on Cornwallis Island, is the hamlet of one of the most northerly Canadian communities – only Grise Fjord on Ellesmere Island lies further north. It is the only settlement on this route.

## Resolute 74°42'N  94°50'W
### Qausuittuq *'place with no dawn'*
With an average yearly temperature of –16.4°C Resolute is one of the coldest habitations in the world. After earlier occupation by Dorset and Thule people, it was only settled again in a

somewhat controversial relocation of Inuit in 1953. While there was already a weather station and military presence, Inuit were brought forcibly from Quebec as part of Canada's pursuit of formal sovereignty. After uncertain beginnings, the incomers learnt to take advantage of the wildlife, but survival on local resources was hard earned. After much heart-searching the Government paid compensation and made a formal apology to the Inuit. By 2006, the population was 229.

Today, Resolute is home to much military training activity. The airport serves as a hub. There are four hotels, including the Qausuittuq Inn, run by Inuit. There is an RCMP detachment, school and the usual services including the Tadjaat Co-op, which will rent you a snowmobile. There's not much in the way of public transport, but you can walk on the gravel roads. Resolute is the starting point for the Polar Race and the Polar Challenge, in which teams race 600km to the north magnetic pole. In 2007 a British team became first to reach the magnetic pole by heavily modified car, beating a sledge-dog team. In publicising their achievement, they tactfully omitted to use the word 'magnetic' in claiming to have reached the North Pole!

Once past Resolute the way to the Beaufort Sea is direct along a deep waterway but it is far from easy, meeting ever more challenging ice. A detour south of Banks Island by the Prince of Wales Strait is possible, but only global warming is likely to make the big-ship passage a realistic one, and then only in high summer.

While the Parry Channel represents the only practical route for a big-ship passage from North Atlantic to Pacific, Roald Amundsen chose to thread his way along a route which has become the choice of subsequent expedition vessels, seeking to avoid the major ice problems. In 1903, at the beginning of the voyage that saw him become the first to complete the transit, he entered by Lancaster Sound, then stopped at Beechey Island to pay his respects to Franklin. He then turned south into Peel Sound, his route involving narrow, shallow and treacherous channels, making it impractical for deep-draft vessels but offering the hope of easier ice conditions.

In a minor but more convenient variation of Amundsen's route, most expeditions turn south a little earlier nowadays, into Prince Regent Inlet, with a chance to approach one of the most bird-rich of the Arctic islands.

## Prince Leopold Island 9km NNE of Cape Clarence, 73°54'N 90°10'W

Lying some 12km off the northeastern tip of Somerset Island at the junction of Prince Regent Inlet and Barrow Strait, this was first sighted in 1819 by Parry, who named it in honour of His Royal Highness Prince Leopold of Saxe-Coburg and Gotha, later first King of the Belgians. (Geographical names have always been a convenient way of recognising sponsors and Parry knew the drill.) As you approach the island there are very often first-year ice floes which provide convenient loafing places for parties of Brünnich's guillemots (known in North America as thick-billed murres).

Prince Leopold Island has spectacular vertical cliffs of sandstone and limestone that rise 265m above sea level. There are shingle spits off the south end, otherwise it enjoys steep-to-vertical walls of rock lifting from deep water. Vegetation is sparse – mosses, lichens, grasses and a few dwarf shrubs. There will be a swarm of auks wheeling about in the sky. Occupied from early May to the end of September, the exposed cliff ledges support a truly astonishing number of breeding seabirds. Auks jostle in serried ranks. Kittiwake nests

## Auks

Auks – guillemots or murres – come ashore only to breed on cliffs and cliff-slopes. At their breeding places they congregate in noisy clusters, standing upright in penguin fashion. Hunting prey they use their wings to 'fly' underwater in hot pursuit of small fish and plankton. Their wings are short and paddle-like, and their flight in air – though they are somewhat reluctant to fly at all – is fast, furious and direct.

The Brünnich's guillemot, or thick-billed murre, *Uria lomvia* is the most ice-dependent of the guillemots, well established around Baffin Island but hugely represented in the Bering Sea, where colonies may involve over a million birds. It has a curious white stripe on the cutting edge of the mandible.

It is an expert diver and underwater swimmer with a diet almost exclusively of fish such as the juvenile form of Arctic cod, capelin, sandlance and squid, taken in deep dives. The murre cities are on exposed cliffs, where the birds occupy ledges protected from the depredations of Arctic foxes by sheer inaccessibility. Amazingly, the chick leaves the narrow ledge when it is only half-fledged, two or three weeks after hatching; it is totally unable to fly. Encouraged by its mother, it launches itself in a perilous fluttering fall to the sea below. Once safely afloat it joins its father and they begin the long migration journey. At this time the adult male is also flightless; he moults as he swims south, escorting the growing chick.

are cantilevered out from the narrowest ledges. Glaucous and Thayer's gulls occupy slopes on the cliff top. The combined sounds of the screaming gulls and the ground bass of the auks provide a musical accompaniment.

The Prince Leopold Bird Sanctuary is recognised by UNESCO as an internationally significant site. Vessels may not approach closer than 5km from the shore without authorisation. Probably the most important bird reserve in the region, it supports a colony that includes the second largest breeding congregation of northern fulmars in Canada. Approximately 20% of the fulmar population, as much as 11% of the Western Atlantic black-legged kittiwake population and substantial numbers of the North Atlantic Brünnich's guillemot population and of the global black guillemot population are found here. Other species known to breed on the island include Atlantic brant, common raven, common eider, Arctic skua, glaucous gull and snow bunting. The total number of seabirds is almost 200,000 pairs. Inevitably, the colony also supports a complement of predators – peregrines and gyrfalcons, as well as the ubiquitous glaucous gulls.

In late summer kittiwake chicks are near fledging. Auk chicks will be about three weeks into their fledging period and totally unable to fly, but, like the guillemots, they will be leaping from the ledges, maybe nudged by mother and encouraged by father, to fall, half flying, half fluttering, to the sea below. There they are joined by father, himself in the beginning stages of moult, to swim south with the Labrador current to winter off the Grand Banks. Sadly a number of chicks will fall foul of the rocks or the ice floes and lie lifeless for the gulls to scavenge. Everywhere on the surface of the sea there will be parties of auks, complete with associated chicks. With luck, there will be ivory gulls, ethereal spirits.

## Glaucous gull

Glaucous gulls *Larus hyperboreus* keep station with any ship on any journey in the Passage. They are happy to take

scraps or perch fearlessly on the rails. Big birds, they are larger, heavier and paler than the familiar and similar-looking herring gull and even more aggressive.

Breeding in the high Arctic, they tend to patronise settlements, especially in association with barnacle goose grounds or kittiwake or auk colonies, which all provide convenient prey. These gulls are omnivorous scavengers, but in the breeding season sustain themselves mostly by piratical pursuit of other birds. Adult dovekies are caught in flight and eaten whole. Eggs and young of auks and kittiwakes are taken from their cliff ledges, or in flight as chicks make their first perilous jump from the nest ledge. The gulls lie in wait under a cliff-face for those chicks which fall to the ground and have to run the gauntlet from the cliff base over tundra to the sea. They also rob eider and fulmar nests for eggs and chicks. Storm-tossed mussels may be taken on the beach, where the birds will also search for fly larvae in decaying weed.

Glaucous gulls may be confused with the equally common Thayer's gull *L. thayeri*, but this has a greyer back and upper wing, with black primaries; the similar-sized herring gull has a dark eye!

Birds from the Canadian Arctic are either resident or migrate south to the eastern seaboard. Alaskan birds migrate to the Great Lakes and some may even reach Mexico.

# Gyrfalcon

The gyrfalcon *Falco rusticolus*, the largest and most northerly of falcons, is another truly Arctic species, well established in Nunavut. A coastal and inshore bird, it holds vast territories; there is always the chance of finding one perched high in the rigging of a ship, keeping a watch for likely prey. They hunt fast and low in sparrowhawk fashion, taking auks, gulls and terns by surprise, sometimes by aerial stoop. Once safely on the ground (or on board a ship!), they break the neck or tear the head off their prey. In autumn they take advantage of flocks of small migrating birds such as buntings. In winter they spend much time on sea ice, far from land.

*Gyrfalcon at home, painting by Keith Shackleton.*

## Ivory gull

The ivory gull *Pagophila eburnean* is whiter than white, with a stout pale-yellow bill, a red eye-ring and short black legs, somewhat larger than a kittiwake. A truly Arctic species, it spends its whole life above 70°N. It is one of the very few birds (others include the ptarmigan and snowy owl) which reacted to the last ice age by adapting to the severe cold and winter darkness, remaining year-round while most birds migrate south. The webs between its toes are much reduced, by comparison with other gulls, to minimise heat loss. Its claws are curved to improve their grip on the ice, for the ivory gull is closely associated with ice in all its forms.

Ivory gulls are principally scavengers. They tend to concentrate along the ice edge, especially near the pupping grounds of seals, where they find sustenance in afterbirths and dead pups. They are heavily dependent on the pickings from polar bear kills, keeping company with the bears in order to benefit from the remains of flesh and blubber which litter the killing ground. They follow dog teams and patronise human habitation in the hope of hand-outs.

## Prince Regent Inlet

A body of water between Somerset Island and the Brodeur Peninsula; to the south, the inlet leads to the Gulf of Boothia. The northern portion is approximately 65km wide, the southern about 105km. The inlet is deep throughout and there are no islands within it. But this is an area where there are likely to be icebergs, finding their way down from the

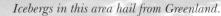

glaciers and land-fast ice of Greenland. Mostly they will be the flat-topped tabulars – check the groups of glaucous gulls for possible ivory gulls. These are waters which will see migrating bowhead whales. They may pass close by a ship, cavorting in parties of dozens. Belugas are somewhat more commonly seen. They come to these waters to moult at the end of their breeding season in Baffin Bay. And even more exciting, there may be narwhals: the gap between ship and ice may force them to pass close by, 'porpoising' as they go.

## Fort Ross

An uninhabited former trading post at the southeastern tip of Somerset Island, Fort Ross is reached just before the eastern entrance to the Bellot Strait. Founded in 1937, it was the last trading post to be established by the Hudson's Bay Company for the fox-pelt trade, operational for only 11 years before severe ice conditions rendered it uneconomical and difficult of access.

Two buildings remain: the factor's residence and the store, still used as shelters by Inuit caribou hunters from

Taloyoak. The main building is in rather a sorry state, but its basic fabric remains fairly sound. It was once a decidedly grand house. Surviving furniture includes a stove, an ice box and two splendidly grotty armchairs. The ventilation system, with adjustable flaps between rooms at floor and ceiling level, is very well organised for an Arctic winter; the central stove could heat the whole building.

There are signs of other buildings, probably accommodation for locals trading with the Company. Several tent rings (circles of rocks which served to hold down the skirts of temporary skin dwellings) are probably from camps of local traders. There is a bronze memorial plaque, placed in 1979 by descendants of Francis McClintock, commemorating his involvement in the Franklin affair.

## Bellot Strait 71°59'N 94°024'W (E entrance)

First to 'discover' this waterway was Canadian Captain William Kennedy of the ketch *Prince Albert*, on the second of the private expeditions financed by Lady Franklin in an attempt to discover what had happened to her husband. Kennedy named the strait after his shipmate Joseph René Bellot. In February 1852, Kennedy and Bellot set out from their winter quarters in Batty Bay – on the east side of Somerset Island – on a dog-sledging survey. Travelling south, they sledged over the ice of the strait which divided Somerset Island and the Boothia Peninsula. They then continued west to cross Prince of Wales Island, returning to Batty Bay via Peel Sound and Cape Walker – a total trek of 1,800km in an unsuccessful search for Franklin. As we have seen, Bellot is remembered by a memorial on Beechey Island; his narrative of the expedition was published posthumously in 1854.

It was not till 1937 that the strait was first crossed by sea by the Hudson Bay Company schooner *Aklavik*, commanded by Captain Scotty Gall. The 20km waterway connects Prince Regent Inlet with Peel Sound and Franklin Strait. It resembles a fjord, 1km wide at its narrowest point, with soundings between 17m and 380m in mid-channel and steep slopes on either side. The north side rises to approximately 450m and the south shore to about 750m. In geological terms the Precambrian rocks (more than 2½ billion years old) are the core of the northern landscape, part of the Canadian Shield, some of the oldest rocks in the Americas.

Bellot Strait is navigable from about mid-August to the end of September. Strong tidal streams mean that the current can run up to 8 knots. Ice can be a real problem: the strait is often filled with bergy bits (more than one metre and less than 15 showing above water), and either entrance may be choked for days on end. 'Mariners should exercise extreme caution,' says the pilot book. 'Passage of the strait without icebreaker assistance is not advisable.' Nowadays, with superb satellite chart assistance and ice information, well-found and well-manned expedition vessels work the strait frequently, but always at slack water (the period of still water around the turn of the tide) and with great respect.

Despite its name, Halfway Island is passed two-thirds of the way through, with Point Zenith on the port hand, the northernmost point of continental America. Strong currents, violent tidal rips and eddies ensure that the formidable Magpie Rock hardly uncovers even at low water. Leading marks reveal the safe channel north of the rock.

Passing through the strait taking advantage of slack water takes a good hour. Loons, eiders, narwhals, harp seals and belugas are all possible sightings, along with the inevitable mosquitoes, which also prefer calm conditions.

## Narwhal

Narwhals *Monodon monoceros* are most abundant in the Baffin Island area, usually in small single-sex gams, but at courting time in spring there may be many thousands off Bylot Island. Close relative of the beluga, it is one of the world's most striking animals and it spawned, by virtue of its long, spiralling tusk, the myth of the unicorn.

Richard Hakluyt, in *Purchas his Pilgrimes* 1624, gives this early description:

> A Sea monster, having a horne, had therewith stricken against the Ship, with most great strength. For when we set the ship on the Strand to make it cleane, about seven feet under water wee found a Horne sticking in the Ship, much like for thickness and fashion to a common Elephant's tooth, not hollow, but full, very strong hard Bone, which had entered into three Plankes of the Ship, that is two thicke Planes of Greene, and one of Oken Wood, and so into a Rib, where it turned upward, to our great good fortune. It struck at least halfe a foote deepe into the Ship.

The male narwhal may measure 4.7m, including its tooth, the female about 4.15m. Average weights are 1,600kg for the male and 900kg for the female. Only the male sports the extended tusk; the longest yet recorded is 2.7m. It emerges from the left side of the upper lip, spiralling clockwise, and totally straight. In fact, there are two teeth, but the second rarely erupts from the mouth. When the whale breaks the water's surface to blow, at intervals of about a minute, the tusk is revealed first, followed by

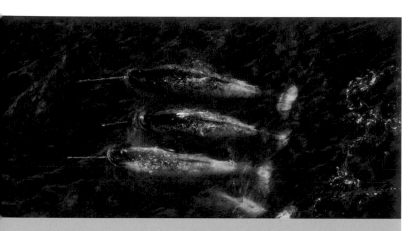

a dark blotched back with no dorsal fin. The function of the tusk has been the subject of much controversy. It seems clear that as a male characteristic it is used in display, establishing dominance in sexual rivalry. When two males 'cross swords' at courting time, the tusk is a weapon and fights are frequent – sometimes the tip is broken. It has been suggested that the animal spears fish with it, but how would it then get them into its mouth? Much more likely is that the tusk makes furrows through the bottom sediment, flushing flatfish. The tusks become worn at the tip, supporting this theory. However, the female narwhal, which has no tusk, fishes effectively and survives perfectly well without one. Flounders are certainly preyed on; the whales also take Greenland halibut, polar cod, crustaceans and squid.

For centuries narwhals were hunted for the ivory tusks which had great value as spears, as status symbols and, in theory at least, as aphrodisiacs. A regulated subsistence hunt continues today: the Inuit use narwhal meat to feed their sled dogs; they use the sinews for sewing thread and, as with belugas, process the blubber into the delicacy *muktuk*. While the population appears stable, the narwhal is seen as vulnerable to climate change because of its limited geographical range.

# BELLOT STRAIT TO CAMBRIDGE BAY

*King William Island. Taloyoak. Amundsen's winter harbour, Gjoa Haven. Queen Maud Gulf Bird Sanctuary. Cambridge Bay.*

Safe emergence from the awesome Bellot Strait brings you to the Franklin Strait, about 160km long and between 80km and 130km wide. This region has never been comprehensively surveyed. Charted portions show soundings as shallow as 10m. Ships drawing up to 9.1m have had success, but passage is made very difficult by the high concentration of sea ice. Most of the year the strait is blocked by ice which comes from the Beaufort Sea by way of Viscount Melville Sound and the McClintock Channel. Even in high summer there will be ice – anything from the frazil which marks the beginning of the freeze to pack-ice floes and dense multi-year ice. You may enjoy anything from subtle tinkling as the cutwater brushes aside a crust of floating ice to explosive crashing as the ice knife of a mighty icebreaker tackles a ridge. Break-up begins in late July and continues to late September, when it starts to freeze again. The window of opportunity for expedition vessels is narrow and hugely dependent on satellite information. In difficult years, icebreakers take advantage of helicopters which allow ice pilots to fly overhead, seeking out leads.

With luck and a modicum of open water this area is prime country for wildlife sightings. As the ship navigates with care in waters decorated with varying amounts of sea ice, from loose floes to heavy pack, there will be birds and mammals. Fulmars will be keeping station with the ship, dipping to enjoy titbits from the plankton churned up by the wake. Glaucous gulls keep them company, sailing on the updrafts and hoping for hand-outs. There will be kittiwakes and perhaps black guillemots. On the floes there will be ringed seals. And where there are seals there is the chance of a polar bear. Once sighted, and if the ship slows to drift, a bear is likely to come to investigate, doubtless encouraged by the galley smell.

The Franklin Strait leads to the wide-open Larsen Sound and Victoria Strait. These too are hazardous waters, much endured by the explorers of the 19th century. It was not till 1967 that the Victoria Strait was crossed successfully, by the Canadian coastguard icebreaker *John A Macdonald*. In fact these are the very waters where the historic vessels of the doomed Franklin expedition finally came to grief. Many of the channels and straits are ice-choked throughout the summer, as Franklin discovered in 1847 when *Terror* and *Erebus* were beset in consolidated ice off King William Island.

**James Ross Strait**, 180km long and 50–65km wide, runs between King William Island and the Boothia Peninsula and contains the Clarence, Tennent, Beverley and Matty Islands. Ice conditions need to be highly favourable for a ship to pass this way round King William Island, but there are worthwhile landings.

## Taloyoak 69°19'N  094°16'W

This is the settlement at the head of Spence Bay, entered by way of Cape Farrar. The Inuktitut name may mean '*large hide*', describing an ancient stone hide or blind used by hunters to herd caribou for the kill. On the west coast of the Boothia Peninsula, with a population of 900, Taloyoak is at the heart of the Northwest Passage. The area has a long history of exploration, including the John Ross expedition of 1832 that resulted in the pinpointing of the north magnetic pole.

Present attractions are primarily its landscape, history and wildlife resources. All-terrain vehicles and foot trails provide easy access to popular fishing and camping spots at nearby lakes. Artists, carvers and artisans are well established, creating 'mystical' carvings in bone, ivory and stone. Spence Bay 'packing dolls', models of Arctic animals carrying their young in *amautiit* (hoods of traditional Inuit parkas), contribute to the local economy.

Since 1934 ship-borne freight has arrived annually courtesy of the Northern Transportation Company, which carries cargo to the hamlets between Prudhoe Bay and Taloyoak, as well as serving oil and gas operations and the mining industry. The NTCL has pretty much a monopoly, protected by the ice which deters competition.

## King William Island, Cape Felix  69°71'N 098°25'W
## Qikiqtak

The landing at Victory Point is characterised by shingle ridges. Even in the damp areas there is little vegetation. It is a desolate and inhospitable place. There is a small memorial to Franklin's men, though by 2012 the exact location of Franklin's grave was still unknown.

## Gjoa Haven  68°37'N  95°053'W

**Uqsuqtuuq** *'lots of fat'* (from the abundance of blubbery sea mammals in the nearby waters)

A hamlet – the only settlement on King William Island, named by Roald Amundsen after his sloop *Gjøa*. In 1903, Amundsen entered Lancaster Sound in pursuit of the first successful transit. By September the weather in Larsen Sound had worsened and the sea began to freeze; he sheltered *Gjøa* here on the southeast coast of the island. By 3 October he was locked in. He was to stay, wintering over, for nearly two years, in what he called 'the finest little harbour in the world'.

He spent time with the local Netsilik Inuit, learning Arctic survival skills:

We had become so accustomed to the cold that it did not bother us much. We were also very well dressed. Some of us wore complete Eskimo costumes, others partly civilised clothing. My experience is that in these parts in winter the Eskimo dress is far superior to our European clothes. But one must either use it alone or not at all. Any combination is bad. Wool underwear gathers all perspiration and will soon make the outside clothing wet. Dressed entirely in reindeer skin, like the Eskimo, and with the clothing loose enough on the body to let the air circulate between the layers, one will as a rule keep the clothing dry. If one is working so hard that the clothing becomes damp in spite of everything, skin dries much easier than wool. Also wool clothing becomes dirty easily and loses its warmth. Skin clothing keeps nearly as well without washing. A further great advantage of skin is that you feel warm the moment you put it on. In woollen things you have to jump and dance like crazy before you get warm. Finally, skins are absolutely wind-proof, which is of course a very important point.

*Amundsen posing in a studio.*

He learnt about Inuit travel and living off the land (his dog-sledging experience in particular proved invaluable in his later dash for the South Pole); he explored the Boothia Peninsula, sledging with his crew, taking measurements and confirming the current location of the ever-moving magnetic pole. He also socialised with the locals (some of the present Inuit of Gjoa Haven claim to be descendants of Amundsen or of his crew).

Amundsen left Gjoa Haven on 13 August 1905, motoring (he had a small petrol engine) through the treacherous straits south of Victoria Island, and from there headed west towards the Beaufort Sea. By October he was again iced in, this time near Herschel Island in the Yukon (see page 37).

The growth of a permanent settlement at Gjoa Haven mirrors the long-term movement of the traditionally nomadic Inuit people toward a more settled lifestyle. In 1961, the town's population was 110; by 2001 it had reached 960 and by 2006 it was 1,064, growing as people moved from the traditional camps to be close to health-care and educational facilities. A number of them are Inuit artists, working with musk-ox horn, whalebone and ivory; also with soapstone, sometimes translucent, sometimes dark green or black. Their work is on sale at the Kekertak Co-op. A local women's group, Quqmaq's, sells finely crafted parkas and *kamiit* (sealskin boots). There is a very good hotel, named inevitably after Amundsen. The community is served by the Gjoa Haven Airport and by annual supply ship.

The area is also home to CAM-B, a North Warning System site. This is a joint US and Canadian radar system guarding airspace across their polar region. It replaced the Distant Early Warning Line – DEW line – system in the late 1980s.

Just south of Gjoa Haven is the Rasmussen Basin and

the entrance to Chantrey Inlet. In 1833–5, Captain George Back, searching for news of the 1832 John Ross expedition, discovered and mapped the Back River (formerly Great Fish River), which reaches the sea here.

## Chantrey Inlet 68°18'N 095°53'W

**Tariunnuaq** *'the people of the place where there is soapstone'*
About 100km long, this is the historical territory of the Utkuhiksalik, nomadic Inuit who lived in snow houses – igloos – in winter, tents in summer, and whose diet centred on lake trout, Arctic char and caribou. Arctic char *Salvelinus alpinus*, *iqaluk* in Inuktitut, is both a freshwater and saltwater species. No other freshwater fish is found so far north. Nowadays the area is a mecca for anglers, most of whom arrive by chartered bush-plane; they have taken record-sized specimens of 9kg or more. Fishing permits are required throughout the region.

George Back reached the **Simpson Strait** in 1834, but did not name it. In 1836, the Hudson's Bay Company wanted 'to endeavour to complete the discovery and survey of the northern shores of the American continent'. Peter Warren Dease commanded an expedition that reached the strait in 1839; he named it in honour of Thomas Simpson, his principal surveyor. It is a shallow and navigationally difficult waterway, notorious for its shoals and tidal rips. Some 65km long and 3–16 wide, it separates King William Island from the Adelaide Peninsula and leads to the gulf which Amundsen named after Queen Maud of Norway as he entered it after the two years ice-locked in Gjoa Haven.

## Queen Maud Gulf

This is a wide and shallow basin, plagued by coastal shoals and enduring severe ice conditions, a consequence of the drift of cold water from the Victoria Strait. Ice cover is complete for about nine months of the year, with many of the channels remaining ice-choked throughout the summer. Consolidated ice being built up into pressure ridges tends to delay the July break-up, then the freeze begins again by early October.

Whales are rare, except for the occasional killers which might be in pursuit of the equally occasional narwhal. Ringed seals and polar bears are the only marine mammals known regularly in these waters. The extent of land-fast ice, their preferred breeding habitat, suggests that the region probably harbours quite a high density of seals, whose presence accounts

## Ringed seal

Smallest and most abundant of the Arctic seals, the ringed seal *Pusa hispida, netsik* or *nattiq*) has a dark grey back marked with grey-white rings; the underparts are generally an unspotted silver. It is shy, with good reason, since it is the favourite prey of polar bears.

Pregnant females dig a den in the fast ice or in deep snow, its main function to give the pup a relatively warm place in which to fatten, since foxes and bears are capable of smelling them at a distance. The pup is born in late April or May, with a white woolly coat. Unusually for seals, it is not weaned for as much as two months, by which time it has shed its natal coat for its first swimming suit of silver.

Ringed seals maintain a year-round breathing hole, scratching with sharp claws through as much as 2m of solid ice. They feed on marine invertebrates and under-ice fauna, mainly crustaceans and polar cod. They suffer much from hunters but nevertheless the average life span can be 15 or 20 years. Arctic foxes, killer whales, for the polar bears. There will be a lot of birds, but the gulf is wide. With luck, a stream of literally thousands of ducks may pass a ship. Among the fish, Arctic char are abundant enough to support a commercial fishery.

The coastline of Queen Maud Gulf is regular, with moderately high rolling headlands, gently sloped beaches and sandy tidal flats. There are a lot of islands, islets, inlets, passages and bays. Cliffs reach 200–300m. Drumlins and eskers are typically found along the coast and inland, reminders of the vast glaciers which have only recently retreated. Drumlin comes from the Gaelic *droimnín*, 'little

Greenland sharks and glaucous gulls take some, but the main predator is the polar bear. They have also been exploited by the Inuit for meat, lamp oil, clothing and for kayak skins. John Ross understood the locals' enthusiasm: in an account of his travels written in 1835 he remarked:

> The meat of these young animals is tender and free from oiliness but it certainly has a smell and a look which would not have been agreeable to any but very hungry people like ourselves. We also considered it a great prize on account of its blubber, which gave us fuel sufficient for cooking six hot messes for our whole party, though the animal only weighed thirty pounds in the whole.

## Canada goose

The Canada goose *Branta canadensis* is unmistakable with its white cheeks on a 'stockinged' black head and neck and its brownish-grey body. It is native to North America, but has a confusing number of subspecies. In the Baffin area, *B. canadensis hitchinsii* was first described by John Richardson, surgeon-naturalist on the first two of Franklin's overland expeditions in the 1820s. In the Mackenzie Delta area, Percy Taverner, distinguished ornithologist at the National Museum of Canada from 1912 to 1942 and author of *The Birds of Canada*, first described *B. c. taverneri*.

This goose is not choosy about its breeding habitat. In the high Arctic it is a tundra-dweller, but always close to water. The male is brawny and can be very aggressive in defending territory. The female looks virtually identical but is somewhat smaller. Both sexes avoid the winter freeze by migrating as far as California and Florida.

ridge', elongated whale-shaped hills formed by the action of glacial ice on glacial debris or moraine. Esker is from Old Irish *escir* – a long winding ridge of stratified sand and gravel. Eskers are frequently several kilometres long and with their peculiarly uniform shape are somewhat reminiscent of railway embankments.

On the mainland side of the gulf and at more than six million hectares, the **Queen Maud Gulf Migratory Bird Sanctuary** is Canada's largest reserve. Much of the landscape has recently emerged from the sea, a flat plain of Precambrian bedrock, lowlands and countless streams, ponds and shallow lakes overlain with glacial till, marine clays and silts that extend 160km inland. It seems an endless green and brown expanse of flat tundra, with ground-hugging plants supported on a permafrost subsoil. Where there is some water there are wet sedge meadows where clumps of cotton grass wave silky tufts. The upland areas contain lichens, mosses and vascular plants. The whole reserve is a paradise for northern birds. Lapland longspurs and snow buntings are the ever-present passerines, but the place is stiff with wildfowl and waders.

The sanctuary was established in 1961 to protect what were then the only known nesting grounds of Ross's geese, and the nesting/feeding grounds for the largest variety of geese in any single area in North America. It is one of the few nesting areas for both Atlantic and Pacific brant, and summer home for maybe a million Ross's geese – almost the entire world population. There may also be a million and a quarter snow geese.

Thousands of other waterfowl, notably tundra swans, white-fronted geese, Canada geese, common eiders, long-tailed ducks and yellow-billed loons breed, moult or pass on migration in the area. The sanctuary harbours significant

Snow geese.

## Long-tailed duck

The long-tailed duck *Clangula hyemalis* is a common and widespread species. *Clangula* comes from the Latin *clangor* for noisy. The once-ubiquitous and wonderfully rude American name 'old squaw' – an indelicate reference to the birds' garrulous gossiping – is now considered politically incorrect.

These ducks congregate at nesting time around boggy places, tundra pools, rivers, sometimes rocky fjords. At the breeding grounds they indulge in wild aerial displays when the drakes belt out a lusty *ack-ar-de-lak*. They are expert divers for molluscs and crustaceans, sea urchins, small fish and some vegetation, reaching depths of at least 30m, though normal dives are less than 10m in half a minute. After breeding they gather in large numbers before migration. When roosting they tend to gather in large rafts and may be vulnerable to oil spills. Many drown in fishing nets; many more are hunted by shooters when they fly south to escape the high Arctic winter.

populations of shorebirds, including pectoral and semi-palmated sandpipers and American golden plovers. The tundra peregrine, listed as nationally vulnerable, is the third most common raptor in the area after the rough-legged hawk and snowy owl. The reserve includes part of the Bathurst caribou calving grounds, and is home to a large population of musk oxen. Inevitably it was recognised in 1982 as a wetland of international importance under the Ramsar Convention.

An increase in Arctic mineral exploration has resulted in pressure on the Canadian Wildlife Service to permit exploration in the Queen Maud Sanctuary. The service recently recommended that the sanctuary's designation be changed to National Wildlife Area to provide even stronger protection. (Global warming may encourage increased ship traffic, which could affect the sanctuary adversely.) The proposal is currently on hold, pending resolution of other land-use issues in the region.

**Jenny Lind Island** 68°42'N 101°30'W is at the southern end of **Victoria Strait**. It is a small island, but with an easy zodiac landing beach at the site of an active DEW line station.

## Cambridge Bay 69°02'N 105°10'W
**Ikaluktutiak** *'good fishing place'*
Known to the locals as 'Cam', the hamlet was named in 1839 after Prince Adolphus, Duke of Cambridge, by Dease and Simpson of the Hudson's Bay Company. With a population of 1,477 in 2006, it is a transportation and administrative centre for the Kitikmeot region, the most important stop for vessels traversing the Northwest Passage. The Arctic Coast Visitor Centre tends to be the meeting place, offering an excellent selection of maps, informative brochures and exhibits. There are artefacts from the local Inuit, some books, postcards and perhaps coffee and tea.

There are two schools. Cam is also the regional centre for the Kitikmeot Campus of Nunavut Arctic College that in turn oversees the Cambridge Bay Community Learning Centre. There are three churches, Anglican, Roman Catholic and Pentecostal. Businesses in the community include a Northern Store with a Quick-Stop selling KFC and Pizza Hut; the Ikaluktutiak Co-op; a branch of the Royal Bank of Canada

Cambridge Bay.

and a post office. There are two hotels, the Arctic Islands Lodge, run by the Co-op, and the Green Row, operated by Inukshuk Enterprises. There is also a modern health centre and a community radio station.

The remains of Roald Amundsen's schooner *Maud* can be seen on the other side of the fjord. Built in Norway for a somewhat delayed and financially disastrous transit of the Siberian Northeast Passage (the Northern Route) in 1918–20, she was subsequently bought by the Hudson's Bay Company as a supply vessel and renamed *Baymaud*. After springing a leak in 1930, she settled on the beach here at Cambridge Bay, where she was used as a storage depot until she quietly fell apart; today she is a sad wreck. There is a chance that she might be repatriated to Norway, though this plan is resisted by the Canadians.

The beach is a prime place for birding: loons, red-necked phalaropes, stilt sandpipers, snow buntings, Arctic terns and long-tailed skuas are all likely sightings.

*The colourful female grey phalarope.*

Of the three phalaropes, the grey *Phalaropus fulicarius*, known confusingly as the red in America, is the most maritime, but, with the slightly smaller red-necked *P. lobatus*, it is one of the two most seen along the shoreline of the Passage. It is superbly adapted to aquatic life, with lobed webs on the toes. A fearless bird, it is surprisingly indifferent to human approach. Yet another surprise is that the female is larger and more colourful than the dowdy male, an indication of their atypical breeding strategy, in which traditional roles are reversed and the female is the dominant partner.

After a winter at sea they wait at the edge of the sea ice for the spring thaw to reveal the ground on the nesting areas. At this time they have empty stomachs after the long haul of migration and are quick to take advantage of the burgeoning insect life.

Both partners make several nests on marshy tundra, forming neat cups with available materials, always close to water. The female then makes the final choice. She has

## Arctic tern

The Arctic tern *Sterna paradisaea* is the only tern found in the high Arctic. Circumpolar in distribution, breeding north to about 83°N, in breeding plumage it has a dark crown, while the rest of the plumage is a light grey, with long tail streamers. Legs, feet and bill are a dashing scarlet. It will hover and pick insects off the tundra exactly as it hovers and snatches small fish from the sea.

Arctic terns may arrive at the breeding area in May before the snow has melted, gathering in colonies which can involve

previously initiated courtship and the pair bond lasts just long enough for her to provide her mate with a clutch of three or four eggs, which it then becomes his job to incubate. The female promptly abandons him to join a club of other females and non-breeders of both sexes off the coast (although she might mate with another male, leaving him with another clutch to incubate).

Phalaropes feed on insect larvae and other small aquatic organisms, wading at the edge of the pool or swimming in tight circles like a spinning top, encouraging food items to the surface, where they are picked off daintily with the thin, hundreds of noisy and aggressive pairs preparing to nest in the open, on low grassy islands, tundra flats or shingle bars. In June they dig a shallow scrape, mostly unlined, in which to lay between one and three eggs, incubated by both sexes for 20–24 days. The chicks leave the nest a couple of days after hatching. Many eggs and chicks are lost to Arctic foxes and skuas, and doubtless some to the Inuit – they are said to be supremely tasty!

Trespass into a ternery and you must expect to be attacked mercilessly. The birds will not hesitate to mount a spirited attack, diving fearlessly and screaming as they come close, drawing blood from an unprotected scalp. The prudent tern-watcher should carry a lofted stick, held high, for the tern will always attack the highest point of an intruder. It is best to leave them in peace, admiring their mastery of aerobatics.

Towards the end of August they take off for a leisurely long-haul flight to the other end of the planet, wintering in the Weddell Sea in Antarctica – the longest migration of any bird, allowing it to enjoy a life of perpetual summer.

pointed bill. Females migrate south early, leaving males with their broods to follow later. Both sexes move a long way south from the polar breeding grounds to winter at sea on the plankton-rich waters off West Africa and eastern South America. Insubstantial birds they may seem, but in fact they endure rough seas, riding high in the water.

The Cambridge Bay area has always been a hunting and fishing location. There are many archaeological sites, including the cairn-like markers known as *inuksuk*. Barren-ground caribou, musk ox, ringed seal, Arctic char and lake trout have always been the primary food sources.

*An* inuksuk, *feature of the landscape around Cambridge Bay.*

RCMP and Hudson's Bay Company outposts were first established in the 1920s. At this time most Inuit would still have been following the traditional lifestyle, visiting the area and using it for meeting, hunting, fishing and trade, rather than living there permanently. After the Second World War a Loran (long-range navigation) tower was built in 1947, then a DEW Line site in 1955. About 200 Inuit were hired to help in the construction. The military presence and the services and economy this represented acted as a magnet; a permanent community was soon established. Unlike the majority of the radar sites which were abandoned or automated, this one, known as CAM-MAIN, remains part of the North Warning System, manned by about 18 people.

Cambridge Bay will be the location of Canada's new High Arctic Research Station, a year-round, multidisciplinary facility dedicated to exploring Arctic science and technology issues; opening is foreseen for 2017. It will of course serve the political purpose of asserting Canada's sovereignty in the high north as well as concrete research objectives.

# CAMBRIDGE BAY TO HOLMAN

*Umingmaktok, Coronation Gulf, Kugluktuk. The copper story. The Northwest Territories. Amundsen Gulf. Ulukhaktok and the ulu. Arts and crafts. Brown bears, caribou. Arctic plants.*

West of Cambridge Bay is Dease Strait, between Victoria Island and the Kent peninsula. About 160km long, the strait widens from 20 to nearer 65km at its western end, where it joins Coronation Gulf.

## Bathurst Inlet 67°41'N 107°57'W
### Qingaun

Lying to the southeast of the Kent peninsula, this is a deep inlet formed by the Burnside and Western Rivers. There are plans for a deep-water port here: to be known as **Baychimo Harbour**, it will serve vessels of up to 25,000 tonnes. The plans, promoted by a consortium of mining companies, include building an all-weather road connecting the port to the mines over 200km away. (Mining activity is buoyant: the industry contributed $32 billion to Canada's GDP in 2009 and even gold prospects are promising.) However, environmental groups have raised concerns over the impact any road would have on the annual migration of the caribou.

## Baychimo Harbour
### Umingmaktok *'place of the musk ox'*

Best known for its sport-hunting guides, this is a small traditional community that feeds and clothes itself extensively from the surrounding sea and tundra. On the site of a deserted Hudson's Bay Company post, the camp was formed originally as an outpost by Inuit families who wanted to live a more traditional lifestyle. With fewer than two dozen residents, Umingmaktok is one of the smallest permanent non-military settlements in Nunavut. Once there was a school that provided education up to Grade 6. Today, any students are flown to Cambridge Bay to return only for holidays. There is no electricity other than that provided by portable generators; communication with the outside world is by satellite phone. The only access is by sea or chartered aircraft. The landing

## Caribou

This most northerly of all deer *Rangifer tarandus* is circumpolar on the tundra (and is known as reindeer outside America). A small animal, the buck reaches to about a metre at the shoulder. It ranges widely over the tundra and islands, is slow-moving and relatively easy to approach. Unlike all other deer, both sexes sport antlers, those of the males being particularly impressive on such a small body. Those of the females are less generous, little more than forked spikes. Adaptation for the Arctic includes a thick coat and a hairy muzzle. The hairs are hollow, trapping a reservoir of warmed air. Caribou have broad and deeply cleft hooves which splay out for support on snow, and are excellent swimmers. In summer they graze the abundant vegetation of mosses, willows, sedges and grasses, perhaps taking a few birds and bird eggs – even lemmings if they get the chance.

The rut takes place in September or October, when a dominant male holds a herd against intruders until he is exhausted, when lesser males have their chance. Males shed their antlers after the rut and grow replacements in the following spring. Females keep theirs through the winter, shedding after strip divides the community in half. On one side are the old Hudson's Bay Company buildings and the Co-op store, on the other the residential area.

The historic Bathurst Inlet Lodge, once a trading post, is now a hub of commercial and cultural activities. The area around Bathurst Inlet and Umingmaktok could be called the Serengeti of North America, on account of the spectacular caribou migrations. There are ancient Inuit campsites

giving birth to the single calf in May or June. Lactation lasts three months, during which time many calves fall victim to predation by bears and foxes. During the summer months caribou feed almost continuously in order to build up a layer of fat and grow a thick winter coat. They are restless animals, always on the move; impressive long-distance migrations take them south to Manitoba and Saskatchewan for the winter, when they forage for lichens.

In historical times these animals were enormously important to the indigenous people. They provided meat for their families and for their dogs, skins for bedding and clothing (although there is some suggestion that the Chukchi caribou produced finer quality), tents, antlers for tools. The arrival of high-powered rifles has encouraged a tendency to overkill and may even jeopardise survival of the species.

*Alpine saxifrage offers a brief burst of colour in the Arctic summer.*

associated with *inukshuk* game-drive systems. The lodge facility serves eco-travellers drawn to the area's wildlife: musk ox, caribou, Arctic fox, peregrine falcon. There are ringed seals hauled out on the ice, birds such as common eiders, long-tailed ducks, yellow-billed, red-throated and Pacific divers, a variety of skuas and assorted wildfowl – with always the slight chance of a grizzly bear. In high summer there are superb displays of Arctic flowers.

## Johansen Bay 68°26'N 111°59'W

The estuary shore of this bay, on the southern coast of Victoria Island, offers great wildlife possibilities. The abandoned airstrip, deserted DEW line station and unoccupied buildings bear witness to the fact that this is an uninhabited area, except for itinerant hunters. It is prime habitat for loons, ptarmigans and other birds of the high Arctic. Perhaps the best plan here is to zodiac the broad Nakyoktok River towards Tassijuiac Lake, where you should see loons, geese, Arctic foxes and hares. Hunters are likely to have set up temporary camps, carefully surrounded by polar-bear warning devices. There are the sites of old meat safes, food caches constructed of stones. Stone rings mark ancient camping sites. There are musk oxen and the inevitable glaucous gulls hoping for hand-outs.

The mainland south of Coronation Gulf may have substantial diamond and uranium deposits; it has certainly been much exploited for the copper deposits along the coast. Centre of the copper trade is the hamlet once known as Coppermine.

# Skuas

These are large, gull-like seabirds with dark plumage subject to a wide range of variation. They have markedly angled wings, with conspicuous white patches at the base of the primaries. Superficially marked like immature gulls, they are heavier, more robust and menacing in mien, as befits a bird of prey. The name 'skua' comes from the Icelandic *skufr* and is a rendering of their chase-call in flight. Theirs is a piratical nature and they have hawk-like beaks to serve it. They are kleptoparasites – carnivorous buccaneers – chasing other birds, mostly gulls and terns, in the air and forcing them to disgorge their catch. True seabirds, they come ashore only to breed.

Three of the family are common along the Passage: pomarine, Arctic (parasitic) and long-tailed skuas. Pairs form soon after arrival in spring, with a tendency to noisy yelping. Their territory will include a lookout point located on a hummock or something similar. The birds are aggressive in defence of the nest – it is best to allow them a wide berth. Breeding success is dependent on a healthy population of small mammals such as lemmings, though the skuas are happy to take advantage of fish refuse and offal at a settlement.

Outside the breeding season they hunt over open ocean, wintering in the far south of the Atlantic and Pacific.

## Kugluktuk 67°49'N 115°06'W

*'the place of moving water'* (there are rapids nearby)

Known as Coppermine until 1996, this is a hamlet located at the mouth of the Coppermine River in the Kitikmeot Region. It is the westernmost community of Nunavut, with a population of 1,300.

Kugluktuk is an important centre of the arts and Inuit culture. It has one of the very few beach jetties in the Canadian Arctic, making an unexpectedly comfortable landing place for tenders that are more used to beach landings. The Heritage Centre is a good source of local information and it offers a chance to buy igloo carvings and handmade dolls. But unless you get here in spring you will miss the Nattiq Frolics, a week-long celebration that features everything from dancing, feasting and Inuit games to seal hunting and snowmobile racing. The community has the usual services, two schools, a post office, Co-op store and also a Hunters and Trappers Association. In the summer, you can play 18 holes at the seaside Kugluktuk Golf Club!

The surrounding landscape is dominated by the rocky and often barren Canadian Shield. The region has a semi-arid Arctic climate, with very cold winters, light snowfall and summers too cool to permit the growth of trees, apart from the ubiquitous Arctic willow *Salix arctica*, which grows only to a height of a few centimetres. Though other trees, pine and birch, exist in the region, they are always dwarfed and extremely sparse. Plants that do grow during summer months include small shrubs, grass, moss, lichens, blueberries, blackberries and cranberries.

Some 20km from the community is **Bloody Falls Territorial Park**, where the Coppermine River is forced into a narrow channel of vigorous rapids and twisting eddies. The remnants

of winter houses, used more than 500 years ago by the Thule, can still be seen. Other archaeological evidence indicates even earlier inhabitants. Inuit refer to the fishing campsite below the falls as Onoagahiovik, '*the place where you stay all night*' – even today it is an integral part of their lives.

The Coppermine River is designated a Canadian Heritage River for the important role it played in exploration and the establishment of a fur-trade route. Nowadays trappers, who once dealt with the Hudson's Bay Company, sell their pelts to southern auction houses by virtue of purchasing agreements set up by the Government.

Kugluktuk marks the far west of Nunavut. Beyond lie the Northwest Territories.

The 160km waterway of **Dolphin and Union Strait** links Coronation Gulf (the southeastern end of the strait, marked by Austin Bay, which lies in both Nunavut and the Northwest Territories) with Amundsen Gulf to the northwest. *Dolphin* and *Union* were small boats of the second Franklin land expedition (the eastern detachment under the command of surgeon-naturalist Dr John Richardson, whose job, in addition

## Grizzly bear

There is a fair chance of seeing a subspecies of brown bear *Ursus arctos horribilis* – a mix of chocolate brown, tan and sandy buff in colour – on the coastal Arctic tundra. Though closely related to the polar bear, the grizzly is a land-based animal and, unlike the polar bear, it is decidedly territorial, aggressive in defence of its resident females.

As tundra-dwellers, the grizzlies' diet contains a high proportion of plant food. But they will hunt whatever mammals present themselves, from caribou to squirrels, and are partial to salmon. Although they have been known to kill a seal, they are more likely to scavenge the sea ice, taking advantage of the leftovers from a polar-bear kill.

Like its marine cousin, the grizzly is dangerous, more inclined to attack than to retreat.

to his medical duties, was to record and collect specimens of plants, animals and rocks). Frozen, the strait is crossed by barren-ground caribou – the 'Dolphin and Union' herd – to reach Victoria Island for the summer grazing, returning to the mainland for the relatively mild winter.

Within the strait lie several islands, including the Liston and Sutton Islands, historically home to a band of 'Copper

Eskimos' known as the Noahonirmiut. The Inuit who use this area, descendants of the Thule culture, originally had no collective name and have been variously known as the 'people at the end of the world' – because few other aboriginal groups had used the area before – or the Copper Eskimos or Copper Inuit, because they made use of the local copper for tools. The first explorers who ventured into this awe-inspiring, formidable landscape were amazed by the pale skins of the people they encountered. In the early part of the 20th century the anthropologist Vilhjalmur Stefansson coined the name 'blond eskimo' for what may have been half-caste individuals, possibly benefitting from experience of Norsemen or whalers.

The local Inuvialuit say that they have seen the average winter sea-ice thickness reduce from roughly 2m or more in the early 1960s to about 1.2m today. There is also an influx of new creatures from flies to wasps; birds arrive that have not been recorded before and grizzlies roam where they were once a rare curiosity.

Dolphin and Union Strait leads to the Amundsen Gulf.

## Amundsen Gulf

The entire gulf is in the Arctic tundra climate region, characterised by extremely cold winters when temperatures may fall below –30°C. In late winter it is covered in sea ice and impassable. Most of the ice breaks up in July during a normal year, with some areas in the eastern part delaying till August. It is generally ice-free in August and September, though westerlies may bring ice from the Beaufort Sea any time.

Beluga whales, seals, Arctic char, cod and even salmon use the waters of the gulf, salmon having shown up for the first time off Sachs Harbour at the turn of this century, presumably in response to global warming.

## Holman 70°44'N 117°46'W

**Ulukhaktok** *'the place where ulu materials are found'*

This is a small hamlet, population 450, on the west coast of Victoria Island, in the Inuvik region of the Northwest Territories. The large bluff overlooking Ulukhaktok is the source of the slate and copper used to make the knives known as *ulus* which are unique to the high Arctic and give the community its name. Each hill has several prominent *inukshuit* (the plural of *inuksuk*) on the summit.

The English name is in honour of J R Holman, a member of Sir Edward Augustus Inglefield's 1853 Franklin search in *Isabel*. (Inglefield was commissioned by Lady Franklin,

### Ulu knives

The *ulu* is an all-purpose knife traditionally used by women in the preparation of food, but with applications as diverse as cleaning animal skins for clothing and, if necessary, trimming snow and ice as building blocks for an igloo. It was traditionally made from sharp slate found on the bluff and had a caribou-antler, musk-ox horn or walrus-ivory handle and a half-moon shaped slate cutting surface. Today it is still often made with a caribou-antler handle, but sometimes with an imported hardwood called sisattaq. The blade is usually of steel, a material not available to the early Inuit. These *uluit* are still used in the home on an everyday basis but are of course also sold to tourists.

A *kimaqtuut* is a small *ulu* with a 5cm blade used for cutting sinew and cutting out patterns from seal or caribou skins. A 15cm blade would be for general purposes. They come in distinct styles.

who said of him that he was 'an elegant young man with a considerable talent in art as well as seamanship'. Lady F had a keen eye.)

Ulukhaktok is home to the Holman Eskimo Co-op, formed to provide income to the residents of the community by producing arts and crafts. Famous for its prints, it is also involved in retailing, the hotel business, cable television and a post office and is the local Aklak Air agent.

The school is very modern, with an interesting collection of handicrafts and artefacts. In front of several houses in town will be fish and seal skins drying in the sun. There are various types of winter sledge, most of a solid Greenland type,

With the Inupiat (Alaskan) style the blade has a centre piece cut out and both ends fit into the handle. In Canada the blade is more often attached to the handle by a single stem in the centre. The shape ensures that the cutting force is centred more over the middle of the blade than it is with an ordinary knife. This makes the *ulu* easier to use when cutting hard objects such as bone. Because the rocking motion used when cutting on a plate or board with an *ulu* pins down the food being cut, it is also easier to use it one-handed (a typical steak knife, by contrast, requires a fork).

*Uluit* have been found that date back to 2500BC. Traditionally, the knife would be passed on from generation to generation, along with the belief that it held the ancestors' wisdom. Some countries prohibit the possession or carrying of knives where the blade is perpendicular to the handle (intended to limit the use of so-called 'push daggers'). The Criminal Code of Canada, however, contains a specific exemption to this law if the knife in question is an *ulu*.

Holman.

although a few will be the lighter 'Nansen' version. Almost every house has a snowmobile, quad bike or other all-terrain vehicle.

Golfing on the open tundra is a local experience at the most northerly nine-hole golf course in America. Specially crafted woven mats are provided for teeing off the tundra and they warn that you may have to putt around a musk ox. The club hosts the four-day Billy Joss Open Celebrity Golf Tournament in the third week of July every summer. (Billy Joss worked for the Hudson's Bay Company in the early part of the 20th century and is reputed to have brought the first golf clubs into the area.)

As in other small traditional communities in the territories, hunting, trapping and fishing are important parts of the economy, but in recent years printmaking has taken over as the primary source of income. Using lithography, stencilling, stonecut and linocut, local artists have created prints that are prized internationally by collectors and museums alike. They are happy to sell their monoprints (printed on a splendid antique etching press from Saint Louis). The *ulu* is a symbol much used here by artists; the *ulu* bluffs are favourite subjects. Arctic co-ops sell artworks online through northernimages. ca. You can find likely auction prices by going to the Inuit Art section on waddingtons.ca.

In recent years Holman has had to come to terms with mineral exploration and in the process has regained an appreciation for its wild places and culturally sensitive areas where long-gone relatives once survived amid the ice and snow. Some companies have learned to work with residents and this has produced hope for sympathetic development around traditional lands.

## HOLMAN TO HERSCHEL

*Paulatuk, Franklin Bay and the Smoking Hills. Sachs Harbour. Aulavik National Park. Musk oxen. Caribou. Beaufort Sea. Polar bears, walruses. Biggest concentration of belugas. Amauligak. Tuktoyaktuk. Conflict between Inuit hunters and the oil industry. Herschel Island. Bowhead whales, ringed seals.*

**Darnley Bay** is a large inlet on the southern arm of the Amundsen Gulf, 32km wide at its mouth, 45km long and fed by the Hornaday River.

## Paulatuk 69°21'N  124°02'W
*'place of coal'*
With a population of 311, Paulatuk is a hamlet at the head of

Darnley Bay, named after the coal which was found in the area in the 1920s when the community was first settled. It is not accessible by road but there is an airport, Aklak Air offering a service from Inuvik three times a week. An annual sealift from Hay River is provided by Northern Transportation.

The land and its wildlife have supported aboriginal peoples for thousands of years. Recent surveys have identified over 360 archaeological sites. Hunting, fishing and trapping have always been major economic activities.

The Roman Catholic Church arrived in 1935 to open a trading post, eventually taken over by the Co-op in 1954. In the 1950s a DEW Line site was built about 100km to the northeast at Cape Parry, providing a wage-based income. The nearby Cape Parry Bird Sanctuary protects the nesting grounds of thick-billed murres (Brünnich's guillemots).

Printmaking plays an increasing role in the local economy. Services include a two-member RCMP detachment and a health centre with two nurses. Schooling is available up to Grade 11 at the Angik School. There is also a community-learning centre operated by Aurora College. Parks Canada has an office, servicing the Tuktut Nogait National Park, 75km east.

With rolling tundra, wild rivers, precipitous canyons and a variety of wildlife and vegetation, **Tuktut Nogait** *'young caribou'* is one of Canada's undiscovered gems. This remote park is home to the Bluenose West caribou herd, wolves, grizzly bears, musk oxen and Arctic char. Cliffs and canyons support a high density of raptors. Federal national parks legislation bans commercial or sport hunting but the Inuvialuit have the right to pursue subsistence harvesting within the park. Currently, this takes place in the northwestern part and mostly involves fishing for Arctic char, hunting caribou and some trapping.

# Collared lemming

Common over the tundra north and west of Hudson Bay, the collared lemming *Dicrostonyx groenlandicus* is the one seen at the back of beaches and especially around the detritus of deserted settlements. Hamster-like, with a short tail and small eyes, its ears are tucked away in abundant fur. Well adapted to a hard life in low temperatures and deep snow, its claws are enlarged as burrowing tools.

The lemming's main foods are grass and the leaves of Arctic willow. Its dense fur turns white in winter, at which time it does not hibernate but lives along the slopes of raised beaches in a grass nest, composed of a principal tunnel with a series of side tunnels leading to the foraging areas. Provided there is a metre or so of snow above it will keep warm – the nest temperature may be 22°C warmer than the surface.

In favourable conditions, lemmings produce a first litter in March, while they are still under the snow. Subsequent litters of half a dozen young may appear monthly till September. Lemmings need to produce an abundance of offspring, since their chances of survival are not great. A good lemming year, which provides plentiful food for predators, has a profound effect on the breeding success of a number of predators, including the Arctic fox , snowy owl and long-tailed skua.

For reasons which are not entirely clear, lemming populations exhibit a classic three- or four-year population cycle, reaching high densities in what is known as a 'lemming year', only to crash subsequently (not by leaping off cliffs) in a steep decline resulting from food shortage, disease and stress.

The Smoking Hills, a site of major scientific interest, lie some 100km west, at Franklin Bay.

## Franklin Bay 69°50'N 126°00'W

Yet another large inlet in the Amundsen Gulf, Franklin Bay is 40km wide at its mouth and 50km long, and well-known for enduring severe gales in late autumn. Belugas are common here.

The tundra and shore area is decidedly quiet and remote, with the atmosphere of an uninhabited planet. A couple of lakes will be home for tundra swans. But the evidence of scat – animal droppings – confirms that there is life, from lemming to caribou.

Franklin Bay is also a favoured hunting ground for grizzly bears. Shore parties are advised to treat the danger seriously and take an armed guard. Walking over the hummocky ground is not easy, but there is plenty of the ground-hugging, delicate, yet hardy Arctic flora, best seen in early summer. One of the striking features of the permafrost underfoot is the patterned ground where the cycle of freezing and thawing methodically separates the fine material from the coarse, creating polygonal patterns.

From a ship anchored in the bay, it is easy to see evidence of the spectacular **Smoking Hills**, steep cliffs of bituminous shale (with a high sulphur content) burning endlessly. They certainly were familiar to the Inuit, but it was on Franklin's second overland expedition in 1826, charting the coast, that Dr John Richardson first recorded them, incidentally naming the bay after his commander. Richardson noted the acrid nature of the fumes and the fact that they destroyed clothing. He added that the pools in the vicinity were acidic and that the Eskimos considered the water bad. Captain

Robert McClure, aboard *Investigator*, reported seeing the fires in 1851. He thought they were made by the locals to attract attention, until his interpreter reminded him that no fuel was available. McClure then concluded, incorrectly, that the fires were volcanic. In fact the smoke results from spontaneous combustion of the bituminous shales.

The fires have probably been burning for millennia, fumigations rising intermittently along 50km of sea cliffs, some of which reach heights of 100m. Many are single plumes, but in the area of densest activity these coalesce to form broad, dense, multiple plumes. The combustion continues throughout the year. Along the base of the cliffs, eroded by the sea, large mounds of burnt material accumulate; mostly these are pink or bright red (from the haematite formed in the process), sometimes yellow or grey.

The bituminous shales contain large concentrations of pyrite: exothermic pyrite oxidation is the cause of the spontaneous ignitions. Places where new burns are starting are characterised by dark areas at the surface of the bituminous bands which are interbedded with ochre-coloured jarosite. These areas are on steep slopes, and may be warm to the touch. When a depth of only a few centimetres is excavated, there are acrid fumes of sulphur dioxide and steam, and often yellow elemental sulphur begins to accumulate. New burns occur frequently as fresh material is exposed to the oxygen in the air by cliff collapse or slumping.

The smoke emerges from spectacular bocannes – burning areas – which are similar in appearance to the fumaroles associated with volcanic activity. These bocannes become surrounded by bright yellow encrustations of sulphur, which is volatilised with the smoke and steam. Analyses have shown the smoke also carries other elements, including gases and salts containing selenium, arsenic, antimony, vanadium, bromine and calcium – much as the smoke from peat, wood or coal fires contains these elements. The selenium and arsenic are carried long distances.

The effect on animals and plants is significant. Some of the Arctic vegetation is very tolerant, while other species, particularly lichens, are not: they are absent for many kilometres around the bocannes. There are plenty of animals reported in the region; indeed the smoke is used by caribou and musk ox to gain relief from clouds of biting mosquitoes: they may be seen deliberately running through thick smoke. While not harmful in small doses for the visitor, it may be quite unpleasant and irritating to inhale. It is unwise to approach the bocannes closely; the risk of being asphyxiated in a fiery pit is small, but real.

The character of the tundra vegetation changes rapidly as you leave the fumigated region behind – flowers and lichens become more common as the noxious fumes fade.

## Sachs Harbour 71°59'N 125°16'W

### Ikahuak 'where you go across to'

Situated on the southwestern coast of Banks Island (named in 1820 by Parry in honour of the great naturalist Sir Joseph Banks), this hamlet – population 122 – is the only permanent settlement on the island. It was named after the ship *Mary Sachs*, part of the Canadian Arctic Expedition of 1913 which was organised and led by Vilhjalmur Stefansson (an Icelandic-born American citizen claiming Canadian citizenship!) in pursuit of new land in the Northwest Territories. Bulk supplies of food and other items are brought to this isolated community by sea in the summer months. Flights from Inuvik, some 530km to the southwest, operate all year.

## Snow goose

Typically in large flocks along coastal Nunavut and the Northwest Territories, snow geese *Anser caerulescens* are strikingly pure white with black wingtips and pink bills. Yapping like small dogs, they inhabit grassy coastal tundra. After the June-August breeding season, they migrate south to US and Mexican coasts, frequently joined by the smaller Ross's geese *Anser rossi* (see page 85).

Sachs Harbour is the headquarters of **Aulavik National Park**. The Visitor Reception Centre presents the Park and Inuvialuit culture, as well as serving as a focus for community activities. Services include a two-member RCMP detachment and a health centre with two nurses. Most of the town lies within 250m of the shoreline, where the locals indulge in ice fishing in the winter. The community's economy is based largely on hunting, trapping and commercial fishing. There is a goose hunt every spring (they are also held in Tuktoyaktuk and Paulatuk), Banks Island having the largest snow goose

colony in North America. For visiting tourists, the Hunters
and Trappers Association provides outfits and arranges big-
game hunts for musk oxen and polar bears, though bear
hunting may soon be even more restricted. Three-quarters of
the world's population of musk oxen roam the island – 'Musk
Ox Capital of Canada' – and they are subject to a commercial
harvest. Local crafts include the spinning and weaving of
*qiviut*, the musk ox's silky underwool, into fine (and expensive)
scarves and sweaters. Barren-ground caribou and polar bears
are also well established.

On 26 April 2006 the world's first documented wild-born
grizzly/polar-bear hybrid was killed near the town, when an
Inuit tracker called Kuptana led an American 'sportsman' to
shoot a polar bear in a legally regulated hunt. The corpse
had the normal creamy-white pelage, but unexpected brown
patches on back, paws and nose, along with dark panda rings
round the eyes. It also had the flattened face and hump back
of a grizzly. In due course DNA tests showed that the animal
had indeed been conceived by a polar bear that had mated
with a male grizzly. Another similar hybrid was shot in 2010.
Time will tell if this is yet more evidence of climate change,
with the polar bear, deprived of the permanent ice on which
it hunts, forced to venture further and further south, into
grizzly territory, in search of food.

Because of climate changes in recent years, local inhabitants
fear their extensive knowledge of weather patterns may suffer:
quite simply, the weather has become harder to predict. Sea
ice has been breaking up earlier than usual, taking seals –
one of the main sources of food for the town – farther into
the Beaufort Sea in the summer. Salmon are appearing for
the first time in nearby waters. More flies and mosquitoes are
seen, as are new species of birds, including American robins

and barn swallows. And now it seems that the Passage is giving marine creatures an opportunity to expand their range.

*Neodenticula seminae*, a microscopic strand of photosynthesising plankton, is common in the northern North Pacific. It wasn't known in the Atlantic until a survey in 1999 found some in the Labrador Sea, where it is now firmly established. The assumption is that it travelled with a pulse of warm Pacific water, part of the changing circulation patterns in the far north. Pacific zooplankton having made the trip, larger creatures will doubtless follow, displacing or disrupting their Atlantic cousins and potentially transforming the entire food web. A European Union-funded consortium of 17 marine institutes is now monitoring these movements in a project known as CLAMER (Climate Change and European Marine Ecosystem Research).

Arctic warming has also allowed whale traffic through the Passage. Grey whales *Eschrichtius gibbosus* became extinct in the Atlantic some 200 years ago and have since been confined to the Pacific. But in the spring of 2010 one individual turned up in the Mediterranean, off the coast of Israel! Instead of pursuing the normal migration route south from its summer feeding season in the plankton-rich waters of the Bering Sea, it had diverted through the Passage to find itself in the Atlantic and beyond.

In January 2010, the continuing reduction in Arctic sea ice led telecoms cable specialist Kodiak-Kenai Cable to propose the laying of a fibre-optic cable connecting London and Tokyo, by way of the Canadian Arctic, claiming that this would cut nearly in half the time it takes to send messages.

## The Beaufort Sea

Most of the Arctic Ocean is covered by ice up to 4m thick, but

## Beluga

To this day the beluga *Delphinapterus leucas* is legal prey, on a subsistence quota basis, for both Inuit and Eskimo. Throughout Nunavut and Nunavik (northern Quebec), 456 belugas were taken in 2006, according to Fisheries and Oceans Canada figures. The annual harvest is regulated through area and seasonal closures, and by a 'total allowable catch'. Easily trapped because of its requirement to visit breathing holes, the beluga's skin is prized for the delicacy *muktuk*, which is chewed raw, eaten boiled or smoked. The almost transparent blubber is used as a fuel oil for lamps.

The beluga, whose name comes from the Russian for 'white one', is the easiest of all whales to identify, although the slightly greyish white yellows with age. Over 4m long, rotund and robust, weighing over a tonne, it is a sociable creature, rarely alone, and relatively common around the icy coast of Baffin Island and the Beaufort Sea.

It is a talkative species – a 'gam' would be the perfect collective

the heaviest concentration is in the Beaufort Sea, which is also the densest region for ice floes. Confusingly, it can be ice-free in some years, choked full of multi-year ice in others. There is a lot of fog. The sea is named after hydrographer Sir Francis Beaufort of wind-force scale fame. Major rivers feeding it are noun for creatures known to whalers as sea canaries because of their varied and musical vocabulary. They indulge in trills, clicks, squeals, bell sounds, whistles and raspberries, sounds which are heard clearly above the surface.

Belugas may gather in literally thousands to calve and mate. The single calf is born in July in the relatively warm shallow waters of estuaries and fjords. Dark grey-brown at birth, the calf is nursed for more than a year and may remain close to its mother for years, becoming white when it is sexually mature.

Belugas hunt in deep water, diving to as much as 500m for 20 minutes at a time to nuzzle in the silt for invertebrates, bottom fish such as halibut, and capelin, char, cod and lantern fish. Summering in the high Arctic, they migrate south in spectacular numbers to winter in places like Hudson Bay. Although the species is regarded as endangered in some areas, the world population has been estimated at somewhere between 100,000 and 200,000. They may live for 30 years, possibly 40.

the Alaskan Yukon and the Canadian Mackenzie.

Marine traffic is facilitated by a coastal pass which opens to 100km wide in August and September. The coastal region is well surveyed, allowing vessels to navigate relatively close inshore, avoiding the pack edge. But it can be a serious obstacle. In late July 2006 the diesel-electric Russian icebreaker *Kapitan Khlebnikov* (15,000 tonnes, 25,000 hp) encountered multi-year sea ice too close to the coast. It took us seven days to get through a problem patch.

The traditional occupations of fishing and whale and seal hunting are practised here only on a small scale and have no major commercial significance. As a result, the sea supports one of the largest colonies of belugas in the world, and there is no sign of overfishing.

On the other hand there are significant resources of petroleum and natural gas under the coastal shelf. After several decades of exploration Amauligak is the largest potential oil and gas field. Discovered in 1983, it lies some 50km north of Tuktoyaktuk in shallow water. Inevitably, a range of possible developments is being considered.

## Tuktoyaktuk 69°27'N 132°58'W
### *'it looks like a caribou'*

According to legend, a woman looked on as some caribou waded into the water and turned into stone. Reefs resembling these petrified caribou are said to be visible at low water. Commonly referred to simply by its first syllable, Tuk is an Inuvialuit hamlet on Kugmallit Bay, located on the Arctic tree line of the Northwest Territories. Formerly known as Port Brabant, it was renamed in 1950 and the community now boasts a population of 929.

Many locals still hunt, fish and trap. These traditional lifestyles provide seasonal incomes to many families which rely on migrating waterfowl, caribou in the autumn and year-round fishing. Other activities include collecting driftwood and berry-picking. There is a Hudson's Bay Company trading post.

The settlement has been used for centuries as a place to harvest caribou and beluga whales. Unfortunately, between 1890 and 1910 American bowhead whalers brought epidemics of influenza, ravaging the population. The whalers were of many nationalities, but notably Polynesians, recruited on whaling vessels that came around Cape Horn and stopped at the Hawaiian Islands before continuing north. Hawaiian sailors were strong and well accustomed to the sea, ideal for the hard work aboard whaling vessels but perhaps less well adapted to the temperature.

Tuktoyaktuk's natural harbour serves it well as a trading hub for the whole of the Northwest Passage. The long-established Northern Transportation Company is a major employer. The embayed harbour has its problems: in foul weather, storm surges affect sea levels as much as tides. In relatively ice-free summers, storm-induced sea-level increases of up to a metre are common, but on occasion they may exceed 2 metres. These increases are associated with onshore winds, while temporary low sea levels occur in response to strong offshore winds. Negative surges can hinder traffic in and out of Tuktoyaktuk Harbour because of the relatively shallow water. Even moderate high-water levels can force bergy bits of ice high up onto beaches.

The petroleum industry is also a key aspect of the economy. The television series *Ice Road Truckers* featured Tuk as a hard-won destination for road freight. In late 2010, the Canadian Environmental Assessment Agency announced that an environmental study would be undertaken on a proposed all-weather road between Inuvik and Tuktoyaktuk, but there are many problems. Arctic Canada is not a sympathetic environment for roads.

Just 5km west of Tuk is **Pingo National Landmark**,

an area protecting eight nearby pingos in a region which contains approximately 1,350 of them – one of the highest concentrations in the Arctic. These extraordinary ice-dome hills are formed by ground ice which develops when temperatures fall in the winter; they can reach up to 70m in height and up to 600m in diameter.

## Herschel Island 69°33'N 138°57'W
### Qikiqtaruk '*island*'

Herschel Island, 120km², is the northernmost point of the Yukon Territory, rolling tundra terrain that ranges in height up to 182m. It was created from sediments thrust up by a lobe of glacier ice coming from the Mackenzie Valley and moving westward along the coastal plain some 30,000 years ago. There is no bedrock core to the island, which is subject to very high rates of coastal erosion. Its surface heaves and rolls from the effects of frost creep. Although the ocean has been slowly encroaching on the island for centuries, climate change is speeding the process. Scientists predict that within 50 years the remaining evidence of whaling culture and that of its Thule Inuit predecessors, most of which is near the shoreline, will slip beneath the waves.

As is to be expected at these latitudes, the climate is characterised by long cold winters followed by short but intense summers. From November to July the island is locked in ice. The sun doesn't appear above the horizon from late November to mid-January, though there is twilight for a few hours in the late morning and early afternoon towards the end of that period. On the other hand, it enjoys continuous daylight between mid-May and mid-July. Strong steady winds are normal throughout the year. July is the warmest month, with a mean temperature of 7.4°C and an average daytime high of 12.8°C, but it can reach as high as 30°C. January temperatures have been known to fall as low as −50°C.

It is hardly surprising, then, that the resident population is 0. But that was not always the case. The earliest evidence of human occupation unearthed so far by archaeological investigations is of the Thule culture, maybe 1,000 years ago.

The first European to visit the island was John Franklin, who came in 1826 on the second of his overland expeditions surveying the coast. This trip was better supplied and more successful than that of 1819–22, the one in which he lost many men and ended up eating his boots. Franklin named the island after his friend, the astronomer and botanist John Herschel. At the time of his explorations there were three Inuvialuit settlements, using the island as a base for hunting, fishing and whaling with *umiaks* for the bowheads.

The whales were relatively undisturbed in these waters till the late 19th century, when American whalers discovered that the Beaufort Sea was one of the last refuges of the bowhead

## Bowhead whale

Although a truly Arctic species, the bowhead *Balaena mysticetus*, Arvig, once known as the Greenland right whale, is decidedly uncommon. Linnaeus gave it its scientific name from the Greek *mustax*, 'moustache', and *ketos*, 'sea monster'; 'bowhead' comes from its bow-shaped skull.

An average bowhead grows up to 15m in length and weighs between 50 and 100 tonnes. It has no dorsal fin, an adaptation to working under ice. It has a massive bony skull which serves to break through as much as 60cm of solid ice. In surfacing to breathe, it tends to show two distinct curves in profile as it reveals itself for the double blow (typically of baleen whales, its nostrils are separated) half a dozen times in two or three minutes, before sounding for 20 minutes. The tail flukes are thrown high as it slides under. On occasion it may lift the massive head clear of the water, showing a white bib.

Bowheads move north – as far as 75° – to give birth in the spring, when the ice breaks up. They are slow swimmers, feeding on surface plankton at the edge of the pack, at about 3 knots. They have a very large mouth, equipped with the longest baleen plates among the world's whales – up to 3m long – which sieve vast quantities of plankton. Fringes on the baleen plates strain the great gulps of sea as the huge tongue is pressed against them; the catch of krill, copepods and pteropods is retained between tongue and baleen. As the ice advances, they retreat to winter as far south as 55°N.

Their great size, and the fact that they float when killed, made bowheads desirable prey for early whalers (in the days before compressed air was used to keep whale carcasses afloat). Originally abundant in the Davis Strait, they were heavily exploited from the 17th century; by 1912 the long decline in their numbers and the fact that faster boats and improved harpoons made it possible to chase the fast-swimming minke whales meant that bowhead whaling effectively came to an end. In spite of having been protected for over 90 years (local subsistence hunting accounts for only a few), the population is still barely holding its own. There are only remnants in the Davis Strait/Baffin Bay area, perhaps a few hundred. The greatest number is confined to the Chukchi Sea, where there may be some 7,000 or so. Bowheads are an endangered species, yet it has been shown that an individual may live 200 years.

population they had devastated further south. Bowheads were hunted for blubber and oil, but prized for the value of their extra long 'whalebone', the baleen bristles which served as filters for sieving the krill ingested in huge mouthfuls.

Commercial bowhead hunting in the area began in 1889. For the short Arctic whaling season to be profitable it was necessary to overwinter in the area and Herschel Island offered a convenient harbour. In 1890 a settlement was established at Pauline Cove. At the height of the Beaufort Sea whaling period (1893–4) the number of residents was estimated at 1,500, making it the largest Yukon community at that time. In 1893, the Pacific Steam Whaling Company constructed a community house; with a recreation room, offices and storage facilities, it became the most prominent building on the island. In 1896 the company offered the house to the Anglican church, whose congregation worshipped there until 1906.

Herschel Island hosted grand balls, theatrical performances and even sports leagues. Five men died during a baseball game in 1897 when a blizzard struck before everyone could take shelter.

When the Yankee whalers had brought the bowhead whales near to extinction at the end of the 19th and beginning of the 20th centuries, they turned their attention to walruses. The animals were easily taken at the edge of the ice as it retreated north in summer, when an old male might have more than 5kg of ivory. Walruses are prized for their tough skin. It is used for covering umiak frames, requiring less sewing than seal skins because the hides are bigger. In places the skin is as much as 5cm thick, making it a first-class material for use as a rubbing-strake on boats, protecting vulnerable waterline planking from the graunching ice. However, the trade that

*Siberian driftwood on the beach below the Community House – now visitor centre for the Territorial Park – on Herschel Island. When Amundsen wintered near here, off Cape Sabine, in 1905/6, he was delighted with the abundance of material suitable for spars. He replaced Gjøa's gaff ('broken and repaired so many times it was of no further use').*

plundered the ivory of their tusks had a devastating effect on coastal natives, causing much starvation.

Then, in 1907, the whaling market collapsed and the whalers abandoned the island. The RCMP remained, enforcers of the law since 1903, when they had first established their presence in two small sod huts. Over the next few decades, the Inuvialuit moved to the Mackenzie Delta on the mainland.

In 1911, the RCMP purchased the island's assets for $1,500. In 1926 the Northern Whaling and Trading Company constructed a store, warehouse and small shed on the island. These buildings still stand, though in recent years they have been moved inland to get them away from the encroaching sea.

## Walrus

The Atlantic walrus *Odobenus rosmarus rosmarus*, Ugyuk, of the Davis Strait and the eastern end of the Passage is a subspecies of the Pacific version, a larger and more numerous animal. Creatures of the ice, they live on substantial floes in the moving pack. The huge body is topped by a small head with small eyes. They have poor eyesight, but excellent hearing and sense of smell. The remarkable upper canine teeth project down and in the Atlantic grow to as long as 35cm (in the Pacific subspecies they may reach 1m). There has been much controversy in the past about the function of these remarkable tusks; they are  weapons for fighting and defence and they are certainly useful tools when the animal is hauling itself up on to an ice floe. In repose they lean on them.

Walruses are never far from shore, even closer when fjord ice breaks up in July. Sometimes they haul out in fair numbers and lie almost on top of each other, a classic example of *thigmotaxis* – 'bodies in close contact' – but they are highly vulnerable to human disturbance at this time. It is prudent to avoid getting too close to them, especially in a boat, since they are prone to attack or attempt to climb in to join you.

*Oosik* is a term used in Eskimo cultures to describe the baculum (penis bone) of seals and polar bears. The male walrus has the largest baculum of any mammal, as much as 55cm in length. Oosiks, polished and sometimes carved, are used as handles for knives and other tools and sold to tourists as souvenirs. In 2007 a 1.4m-long fossilised oosik from an extinct species of walrus, believed by the seller to be the largest in existence, was sold for $8,000.

The females are sexually mature at about five or six years of age, the males from about seven, though they are unlikely to get an opportunity to mate till several years later. Breeding activity is at its peak in April and May, with a single calf (or rarely twins) being born from April to June. The solo calf enjoys dedicated solicitude from its mother, who offers rich milk and suckles for as long as two years, maybe even longer if she is not pregnant with her next calf. Young breeding females may calve every two years, but older ones have a more relaxed attitude.

Walruses are mainly bottom-feeders in shallow water, diving for several minutes at a time to take molluscs and crustaceans. The tusks may be used to work their way over the bottom, but it is the stiff facial whiskers that feel for the hidden clams. Powerful lips suck out the muscle and siphon, then spit out the shell. Other, less shelly invertebrates and small fish are eaten whole, and it seems that walruses ingest a lot of gritty sand which is duly dispatched from each end, with much belching and farting. When Inuit hunters kill a walrus during the summer months they cut out the stomach, packed with thousands of clams, and bury it until winter, when they retrieve it to feast on the delicacy.

In 1964, the Mounties left. The original community house is still there, believed to be the oldest frame building in the Yukon. It remains in good condition and serves as a visitor centre for the Herschel Island Territorial Park, created in 1987, the year in which the last year-round residents, the MacKenzie family, left. Seasonal park rangers, all of Inuvialuit descent, tell the story of the island and its wildlife.

A small museum reveals the history. There are photograph albums to examine. The adjoining 'bone house' has many relics from the whaling days. The ice houses are worth seeing – natural refrigerators, 2–3m down in the permafrost, their sides made of driftwood, the roofs covered with sod. There are the remains of historic sod huts situated along what was once a main road. At the end of that road is all that is left of the Anglican mission house, populated now by the largest colony of black guillemots in the Western Arctic. There is a cemetery for the indigenous Christians – missionary converts – and whalers, with two graves of RCMP on a small rise. Many of the oldest relics, left by the Thule people hundreds of years ago, washed out to sea in the 1970s and 1980s before they could be excavated. In 1999, a storm hurled ice into one of the old whaling buildings. Park officials moved some structures farther inland. Nothing can be done to save the island's graveyards from the encroachment of the sea.

There are over 200 plant species, found in a diversity of habitats. The vegetation of this eco-region is described as Arctic tundra, with continuous ground cover and no trees. Most of the island is composed of level to gently sloping stable uplands, vegetated by cotton grass, ground shrubs and wildflowers. During the growing season the humid maritime climate fosters a lush growth of tundra flowers, including vetches, louseworts, Arctic lupines, arnicas and forget-menots. From late June to early August there is an explosion of colour.

At least 94 bird species have been counted here, 40 of which breed. The island hosts Arctic terns and American golden plovers. Red-necked phalaropes spin for mosquito larvae on the tundra ponds. Other breeders include the common eider, rough-legged hawk, snow bunting, Lapland bunting and redpoll.

The Porcupine River has its source in the mountains north of Dawson City, Yukon. It derives its name from the Gwich'in word *Ch'ôonjik* – Porcupine Quill River. This is one of the few places on the planet where it is possible to see three species of bear. There are grizzly bears, there are black bears and of course there are polar bears. There are moose and musk oxen. Lemmings, tundra voles and Arctic shrews are common. Red fox and Arctic fox are also known to den on the island.

The coastal waters, fed by the nutrient-rich waters of the Mackenzie River, are a haven for fish and marine mammals. Zooplankton thrive and nourish Arctic cod, char and Pacific herring. Ringed seals are the most common marine mammals, fishing the edges of the ice during the summer. Polar bears are major predators. In summer they live along the edges of the pack ice near the island. In winter, a few female bears den under the snow on the island's northern slopes. Bowhead whales pass as they migrate westward towards the Bering Sea in September, feeding close to the surface on krill. In May 2007, a 50-tonne specimen caught off this coast was found to have the head of an explosive harpoon embedded deep under its neck blubber. The 9cm arrow-shaped projectile had been manufactured in New Bedford, Massachusetts, a major whaling centre, around 1890, suggesting the animal may have survived a similar hunt well over a century before.

The World Monuments Fund has placed Herschel Island on its '100 Most Endangered Sites 2008' watch list, citing 'rising sea levels, eroding coastline and melting permafrost' as imminent threats.

## Arctic fox

Circumpolar and restricted to the Arctic, Arctic foxes *Alopex lagopus* are most abundant in the coastal regions, although they wander freely over the sea ice, happy to follow a polar bear to scavenge the remains of a seal kill. They are much smaller than the red fox of lower latitudes, about 1m in length, of which more than half is tail. The dog is heavier than the vixen, weighing up to 5kg.

With its short, blunt head, small furry ears and thick insulating underfur, the Arctic fox will survive in temperatures as low as −70°C. Terrestrial vertebrates tend to be white if they live in the far north, an adaptation to living with snow, and the Arctic fox is a perfect example, along with the polar bear and the ptarmigan. But in summer in the Canadian Arctic they are mostly greyish-brown.

Rather solitary creatures for much of the year, they nevertheless enjoy a strong pair bond, reuniting at the family den for the breeding season between February and May. The den will be in sandy soil or soft ground, perhaps burrowed into a creek or lake bank, the side of a pingo or a dune ridge. It will have a series of tunnel entrances, and is very often sited alongside a seabird colony which offers a convenient food source. The vixen may breed in her first year, but more normally in her third; she produces an average of seven pups, though as many as 20 have been recorded. They will be weaned by mid-summer, when the abundance or otherwise of food will have a major impact on success. At this time the dog fox will bring food to the den for the pups to learn to tear apart. They

Herschel Island is the exit port from Canada, requiring visiting officials to arrange clearance for the United States.

are cared for through the summer until they disperse to forage and fend for themselves. The foxes may not breed at all in a year when food is scarce.

Given fast ice or convenient ice floes to aid its travel, the fox, which is perfectly capable of swimming short distances, may cover great areas in search of food. On this high Arctic coastline much of the food comes from seabird colonies and tideline carrion. As opportunists, they will eat anything they can get hold of. In a hard winter they will rely to a certain extent on food they cached in the summer.

# HERSCHEL TO NOME

*Herschel to the Pacific. US Territory. Prudhoe Bay. Barrow.*
*Bowhead whales. Ross's gull. Oil. Ice. Chukchi Sea. Bering*
*Sea.*

There is a long-standing dispute over the international
boundary between the Canadian territory of Yukon and the
US state of Alaska. Canada claims the maritime boundary
to be 200 nautical miles out along the 141st meridian – the
Alaska-Yukon land border. The United States claims that the
boundary line is perpendicular to the coast. This difference
creates a wedge with an area of about 3,000km$^2$ that is claimed
by both nations. Both agree that they are bound by the
1958 Convention on the Continental Shelf, which grants a
sovereign state rights over the continental shelf that borders
it; and both agree that the boundary should be 'equitable'.
Significant steps were taken in 2010 in the hope of eventual
resolution, with the two countries agreeing to work together
on a survey of the disputed area.

Behind the coast lie the 7,500ha **Arctic National Wildlife**
**Refuge**, on the Alaska North Slope; and the seeds of serious
controversy. The area contains significant quantities of oil,
ripe for exploitation. It is also home for a porcupine caribou
herd of more than 150,000 animals – an important means
of subsistence for the region's indigenous inhabitants. Some
7,000 Athabascan Indians fear that oil exploration will disrupt
the calving grounds and cause a catastrophic loss of their
most important resource. But while there are natives who rely
on hunting and fishing for much of their daily sustenance,
there are others who look to oil-generated wage employment
as a means to economic livelihood. The Inupiat people are
coastal dwellers who stand to gain employment and benefit

## Porcupine caribou

The porcupine or Grant's caribou *Rangifer tarandus granti*, 'Tuktu' in Inuktitut, is a subspecies commonly found on Herschel Island in the summer. The name derives not from the animal porcupine, but from the Porcupine River, which runs through a large part of its range. Though numbers fluctuate, the herd comprises over 125,000 animals which migrate over 2,500km a year between their winter range and calving grounds, the longest land-migration route of any mammal on the planet. They provide the primary sustenance of the native Gwich'in, who traditionally established their communities in sympathy with the animal's migration patterns. There is currently controversy over whether possible future oil drilling on the coastal plains of the Arctic National Wildlife Refuge will have a severe negative impact on the caribou or whether the population will increase.

from leasing their rich land to the oil companies. The US Government faces difficult decisions.

## Prudhoe Bay 70°19'N  148°42'W
**Sagavanirktok** *'strong current'*

John Franklin, who named it in 1826 after his classmate Captain Algernon Percy, Baron Prudhoe, would rub his eyes if he could see this company town today. At any given time several thousand transient workers support the resident population at the local oil field. Airport, lodging and general store are located close by at Deadhorse; rigs and processing facilities are on scattered gravel pads laid over the tundra, in close communion with nesting loons and gyrating phalaropes. Prudhoe Bay is the northern terminus of the Pan-American Highway, two days from Fairbanks in the Yukon.

## Barrow 71°34'N 155°27'W
**Ukpeagvik** *'place where snowy owls are hunted'*

The settlement takes its modern name from Point Barrow, named in 1825 by Captain Frederick Beechey of *Blossom* in honour of his patron Sir John Barrow of the British Admiralty. Beechey was plotting the coastline of the Bering Strait at the time, but reached well into the Chukchi Sea to its furthermost at Point Barrow.

Unsheltered, battered by pitiless winds and with sea ice pounding the coast, Barrow offers only an exposed anchorage and often an uncomfortable landing. This is one of the coldest places on earth, with over 325 days below freezing and less than 12.5cm of rain a year. Winter weather can be extremely dangerous because of the combination of cold and wind, while summers are cool even at their warmest.

Some 2,000km south of the North Pole, Barrow is the

# Loon

*Red-throated diver.*

Loons, or divers, are aquatic birds adapted to search underwater for fish and molluscs. Their legs are set well back on the body with webbed toes as propellers; they are inevitably somewhat clumsy on land, but are superbly at home underwater.

The common or great northern diver *Gavia immer* is large and heavy-billed with a black head and white collar. The red-throated *G. stellata* has a pale grey head with a red throat patch. It is the smallest, most northerly and most widespread of the divers, best known for their eerie, wailing calls. They have characteristic long necks in flight, with up-tilted beaks while on the water. They prey on small fish, mostly polar cod, butterfish and capelin taken by underwater pursuit.

They are circumpolar, breeding along the coastal fringe on the tundra to 83° N. Arriving north in May, they stay at sea till the ice breaks up on the freshwater lakes and ponds where they nest. They come ashore only for breeding, sometimes in small colonies. In June they go to freshwater pools or large lakes, with a profusion of bankside vegetation. The nest is a flattened patch of greenery or sometimes a mossy, weedy heap, very close to the water so that the birds can slide in and out with ease. If all goes well, newly hatched chicks leave the nest on their second day, already able to swim, cared for by both parents. They fledge at 43 days, when they become independent and migrate, wintering south off both American coasts.

economic, transportation and administrative centre for the North Slope borough. It is the northernmost community, mainly of Inupiat Eskimo, in the United States. Another of the Cold War radar stations of the DEW line was established here in 1957 and in 1958 Barrow was incorporated as a 'first-class city', a designation usually reserved for much larger places.

Exploration by the National Petroleum Reserve and the Naval Arctic Research Lab brought new people to the region so that it had a population of 4,000 in 2009. The oldest frame building in Arctic Alaska is still to be seen at the Cape Smythe Whaling and Trading Station, which was established in 1893. Today Cape Smythe is home for the Wiley Post–Will Rogers Memorial Airport, operated by the Frontier Flying Service from Fairbanks.

The landscape here is tundra, sitting on permafrost that is as much as 400m deep.

The **Pigniq archaeological site** contains 16 dwelling mounds of a culture believed to have existed from AD500–900. These archaeological finds are considered a key link between the Dorset and Thule cultures of Alaska and Canada.

In spring the bowhead whales pass Point Barrow on their migration to the feeding waters of the Beaufort Sea. This is the signal for a legally permitted subsistence hunt using the traditional skin boats – *umiaks*. To make the boats seaworthy, whaling crews have already hunted for *oogruk*, the bearded seal, whose skins are scraped free of hair, sewn together with a waterproof stitch, then stretched over the wooden frame and tied into place using caribou sinew. With a new skin covering the frame, the *umiak* is hauled out into the wind and cold, to dry. In May, when the bowhead whales show up, the skin boats are pulled on sleds by snowmobiles out onto the icy sea. Whale hunts inevitably encourage other local residents such as polar and grizzly bears to congregate for whale-meat feasts along these frigid shores.

*Bearded seal.*

One birding magazine rated Barrow among its top spots nationwide, describing the bird life as spectacular. Snowy owls, Stellar's eider and a cornucopia of wildfowl and waders are seen here. The Barrow Birding Center provides a checklist of 185 species – get a copy from the King Eider Inn.

## The Chukchi Sea

The International Date Line is displaced eastwards as it crosses the Chukchi Sea, for convenience and to preserve the Siberian provenance of Wrangell Island and the Chukotka Peninsula. The sea is named after the Chukchi people, traditionally fishermen, whalers and walrus hunters in this frozen waste.

It is navigable – with due caution – for about four months of the year, but this will be the best opportunity of seeing two rare and beautiful gulls – Ross's and Sabine's.

With luck, as you progress across the Chukchi Sea, walruses will be cavorting around the ship. There may be dozens, accompanied by first-year pups.

## Sabine's and Ross's gulls

Edward Sabine was first to describe the gull named after him, *Larus sabini*, in 1818, when he was ship's naturalist in **Isabella** with Captain John Ross (James Clark Ross, the captain's nephew, was on board as midshipman). Exploring in search of the elusive Northwest Passage he shot and took specimens of an 'elegant forktailed gull – hitherto unknown and undescribed' – from a mixed colony of gulls and terns.

It is a graceful bird, smaller than the kittiwake, roughly the size of an Arctic tern. Light and agile in flight, it has a black hood, black bill with yellow tip and white forked tail. In flight, the upper wing shows a conspicuous white triangle contrasted with black primaries. The dark grey mantle completes a strikingly m-shaped pattern. They hover and dip for crustaceans and small fishes, much in the manner of the terns.

At the end of the breeding season, in late August or September, they leave the marshy islets for a life at sea. This is when they are most likely to be seen off the Alaskan coast.

Small in size but with a black necklace and underparts suffused a delicate pink, Ross's gull *Rhodostethia rosea* is the only gull with a wedge-shaped tail. It is lusted after by every birder, mainly because of its reclusive rarity but also on account of its beauty and graceful movements on the ground and in flight. The taxonomic honour of first describing this species was claimed in June 1823 by midshipman James Clark Ross, sailing with **Hecla**, yet again searching for the

*Ross's gull.*

elusive Northwest Passage. His shipmate Edward Parry recorded in the expedition's journal:

> Our shooting parties have of late been tolerably successful. Mr Ross procured a specimen of gull having a black ring round its neck, and which in its present plumage, we could not find described.

It is a truly Arctic bird, relatively rarely seen south of the Arctic Circle. Its breeding ground was one of the great mysteries of the ornithological world until early in the 20th century. We now know that a few nest on low islets in the Resolute area, on the south coast of Cornwallis Island at the Atlantic end of the Passage, but the main area is further west – in fact every river delta between the Chukchi and Taimyr peninsulas. There Ross's gulls nest on islands in lakes and on tundra swamps some 300km north of the Arctic Circle. After breeding they move along the coast towards the Beaufort Sea coast of Alaska. Until well into the 20th century the Inupiat natives shot Ross's gulls for the pot as they passed Point Barrow towards the end of September.

In this shallow area there is no shortage of prey for the gulls: they feast on the algae which thrive on the underside of the ice floes, on plankton associated with the edge of the pack and on assorted bugs in the tideline detritus of the shore.

This is not in a likely place to spot the polar bears which are common on ice floes. Bears found in this area are from one of the five genetically distinct Eurasian populations. There may be grey whales, minkes and killers. This is one of the few sea areas where bowheads are almost common.

## The Bering Strait

Just south of the Arctic Circle, the Bering Strait is named after Vitus Bering, the Danish navigator who in 1728, working for the Russian Navy in *Gabriel*, was the first European to sail north from the Pacific Ocean to explore the strait. It guards the entrance to the Bering Sea, marked on the Alaskan side by the westernmost point of the North American continent, Cape Prince of Wales 168°05'W, and on the Russian side by the easternmost point of the Asian continent, Cape Dezhnev 169°43'W. It was this relatively narrow strait that encouraged archaeologists to propose that back in the Pleistocene ice age – when ocean levels were lower (perhaps as a result of glaciers locking up vast amounts of water) – an underwater ridge became exposed. This provided a land bridge, Beringia, which nomadic hunters crossed from Asia to populate the Americas.

The Bering Strait links the Chukchi to the Bering Sea and the Pacific Ocean, the climax of the Northwest Passage.

In the **Bering Sea** the interaction between currents, sea ice and weather make for a vigorous and productive ecosystem based on flourishing phytoplankton. Although it is possibly the most dangerous trade in the world, commercial fishing here is big business. On the US side, commercial fisheries catch approximately $1 billion worth of seafood annually, while Russian fisheries are worth approximately $600 million. It is the central location for the Alaskan king crab and opilio crab seasons. Landings from Alaskan waters represent half the US catch of fish and shellfish.

Perhaps 20 million individuals of over 30 species of seabirds breed in the Bering Sea region. Marine mammals include bowhead, blue, fin, sei, humpback, sperm, beluga, killer and the rare North Pacific right whale; walrus and northern fur seal; and last but not least the polar bear.

But there is evidence that climate change is having profound effects in the Bering Sea.

Unusually warm summers reduce the production of high-energy plankton. Studies have shown that there has been a sharp decline in the amount of plankton over the last 50 years. The future for the wildlife of this region is uncertain, especially given the possibility of large-scale oil exploitation.

South of the Bering Sea lies the open Pacific, the goal chased through centuries of exploration with dreams of a short cut from Europe to the Orient – from the Atlantic to the Pacific – across Arctic Canada. In the end, as we have seen, it was the Norwegian Roald Amundsen who sailed through the Bering Strait to confirm success when his little sloop *Gjøa* reached Nome on 31 August 1906. As he put it:

> *Victory awaits him who has everything in order – luck we*
> *call it. Defeat is definitely due for him who has neglected*
> *to take the necessary precautions – bad luck we call it.*

Kapitan Khlebnikov *looking for a lead, seen from the ice-pilot's helicopter.*

# Transits of the Northwest Passage to 2011

Compiled by Robert Headland of the
Scott Polar Research Institute

The earliest traverse of the Northwest Passage was completed in 1853 but used sledges over the sea ice of the central part of Parry Channel. Subsequently the following 160 complete transits have been made to the end of the 2011 navigation season. These proceed to or from the Atlantic Ocean (Labrador Sea), in or out of the eastern approaches to the Canadian Arctic archipelago (Lancaster Sound or Foxe Basin), then the western approaches (McClure Strait or Amundsen Gulf), across the Beaufort Sea and Chukchi Sea of the Arctic Ocean, from or to the Pacific Ocean (Bering Sea). The Arctic Circle is crossed near the beginning and the end of all transits. The routes and directions are indicated in the list below. Complements of a few vessels left them for winter to return in a later navigation season. Details of submarine transits are not included because only two have been reported and they do not need to navigate through ice.

Seven routes have been used for transits of the Northwest Passage with some minor variations (for example through

Pond Inlet and Navy Board Inlet) and one composite opportunistic course (transit 147). These are:

**1:** Davis Strait, Lancaster Sound, Barrow Strait, Viscount Melville Sound, McClure Strait, Beaufort Sea, Chukchi Sea, Bering Strait. *The shortest and deepest, but most difficult way owing to the severe ice of McClure Strait. Because of its depth this is the route is used by submarines. Only one surface transit has used this route, although two other vessels have rounded the western coast of Banks Island.*

**2:** Davis Strait, Lancaster Sound, Barrow Strait, Viscount Melville Sound, Prince of Wales Strait, Amundsen Gulf, Beaufort Sea, Chukchi Sea, Bering Strait. *An easier variant of route 1 which may avoid severe ice in McClure Strait; suitable for deep-draft vessels.*

**3:** Davis Strait, Lancaster Sound, Barrow Strait, Peel Sound, Franklin Strait, Victoria Strait, Coronation Gulf, Amundsen Gulf, Beaufort Sea, Chukchi Sea, Bering Strait. *The principal route; used by most vessels of draft less than 10m.*

**4:** Davis Strait, Lancaster Sound, Barrow Strait, Peel Sound, Rae Strait, Simpson Strait, Coronation Gulf, Amundsen Gulf, Beaufort Sea, Chukchi Sea, Bering Strait. *A variant of route 3 for small vessels if ice from McClintock Channel has blocked Victoria Strait. Simpson Strait is only 6.4m deep and has difficult currents.*

**5:** Davis Strait, Lancaster Sound, Prince Regent Inlet, Bellot Strait, Franklin Strait, Victoria Strait, Coronation Gulf, Amundsen Gulf, Beaufort Sea, Chukchi Sea, Bering Strait. *This route is dependent on ice conditions in Bellot Strait, which has difficult currents. Mainly used by eastbound vessels.*

**6:** Davis Strait, Lancaster Sound, Prince Regent Inlet, Bellot Strait, Rae Strait, Simpson Strait, Coronation Gulf, Amundsen Gulf, Beaufort Sea, Chukchi Sea, Bering Strait. *A variant of* *route 5 for small vessels if ice from McClintock Channel has blocked Victoria Strait.*

**7:** Hudson Strait, Foxe Basin, Fury and Hecla Strait, Bellot Strait, Franklin Strait, Victoria Strait, Coronation Gulf, Amundsen Gulf, Beaufort Sea, Chukchi Sea, Bering Strait. *A difficult route owing to severe ice, usually at the west of Fury and Hecla Strait, and the currents of Bellot Strait. Mainly used by eastbound vessels as an alternative if practicable.*

Complete transits have been made by 114 different vessels. The Russian icebreaker *Kapitan Khlebnikov* has made 17 transits, the largest number of any ship. *Hanseatic* has made 9, *Bremen* 6 (2 under the former name *Frontier Spirit*), four vessels have each made three transits, and 11 have made two. More than one year was taken by 17 of these vessels, mainly small craft, to complete a transit, wintering at various places along the route. The vessels are from 25 registries: 43 from Canada, 24 Russia, 20 United States, 17 Bahamas, 10 each Britain and France, five New Zealand, four each Germany and Sweden, three each Cayman Islands and Poland, two each Australia, Belgium, and Norway, and one each from Austria, Barbados, Croatia, Finland, Ireland (Éire), Japan, Marshall Islands, Netherlands, Singapore, South Africa and Switzerland. Passengers have been carried on 37 transits but only two were otherwise commercial voyages. Several of the vessels have travelled through the Panama Canal and thus circumnavigated North America, two have circumnavigated North and South America, and six have circumnavigated the Arctic Ocean. Captain Viktor Vasiliev, of the Far East Shipping Company, Vladivostok, has commanded eight transits, Captain Heinz Aye six transits and several others have commanded more than one.

Excluding the composite voyage (number 147) a route analysis of the remaining 159 transits shows:

Route 1   west 1 east 0 total 1          Route 2   west 6 east 5 total 11

Route 3   west 26 east 28 total 54      Route 4   west 30 east 12 total 42

Route 5   west 11 east 18 total 29      Route 6   west 1 east 18 total 21

Route 7   west 0 east 3 total 3         All Routes west 75 east 84 total 159

The list is in alphabetical order in the years of completion of the voyages (not by the precedence of completion). Superscript numbers are cumulative numbers of voyages, commands, flags, etc.

Sources include a compilation by Thomas Pullen and Charles Swithinbank published in Polar Record (1991), Brian McDonald (CCG) who has maintained and expanded the record, with advice from Lawson Brigham (USCG), Peter Capelotti (USCG), David Fletcher, Peter Semotiuk, Patrick Toomey (CCG), Victor Wejer, personal observations made during several transits with Quark expeditions, many publications, advice from persons directly involved and several internet sites. Advice of subsequent voyages, any corrections and similar details would be appreciated. It is intended that this compilation will be revised annually.

| | Year | Vessel | Registry | Master | Route |
|---|---|---|---|---|---|
| 1 | 1903-06 | Gjøa (21m auxiliary sloop) | Norway[1] | Roald Engelbregt | West 4 |
| | | Gravning Amundsen Wintered twice in Gjøa Haven and once off King Point | | | |
| 2 | 1940-42 | St Roch[1] | | | |
| | | (29·7m RCMP auxiliary schooner) | Canada[1] | Henry Asbjørn Larsen[1] | East 6 |
| | | Wintered at Walker Bay and Pasley Bay, traversed Pond Inlet | | | |
| 3 | 1944 | St Roch[2] (RCMP auxiliary schooner) | Canada[2] | Henry Asbjørn Larsen[2] | West 2 |
| | | Return voyage, first transit in one season, traversed Pond Inlet | | | |
| 4 | 1954 | HMCS Labrador (icebreaker) | Canada[3] | Owen Connor Struan Robertson | West 2 |
| | | First continuous circumnavigation of North America | | | |
| 5 | 1957 | USCGC Storis (icebreaker) | United States[1] | Harold Lambert Wood | East 6 |
| 6 | 1957 | USCGC Bramble (buoy tender) | United States[2] | Henry Hart Carter | East 6 |
| 7 | 1957 | USCGC Spar (buoy tender) | United States[3] | Charles Vinal Cowing | East 6 |
| | | Travelled in convoy, Storis escorted Bramble and Spar, accompanied by HMCS Labrador from Bellot Strait | | | |

| | Year | Vessel | Registry | Master | Route |
|---|---|---|---|---|---|
| 8 | 1967 | CCGS *John A. McDonald* (icebreaker) | Canada[4] | Paul M. Fournier | West 3 |
| | | *Dispatched to assist USCGC* Northwind *beset 900 km N off Point Barrow with damaged propeller, circumnavigated North America* | | | |
| 9 | 1969 | USCGC *Staten Island* (icebreaker) | United States[4] | Eugene F Walsh | East 2 |
| | | *Escorted oil tanker* Manhattan *on return voyage from Point Barrow* | | | |
| 10 | 1970 | CSS *Baffin* (research icebreaker) | Canada[5] | P Brick | East 2 |
| 11 | 1970 | CSS *Hudson*[1] (research icebreaker) | Canada[6] | David W. Butler | East 2 |
| | | *First circumnavigation of the Americas* | | | |
| 12 | 1975 | *Pandora II* (hydrographic research vessel) | Canada[7] | R. Dickinson | East 7 |
| 13 | 1975 | *Theta* (research vessel) | Canada[8] | K Maro | East 7 |
| | | *Travelled in company* | | | |
| 14 | 1975 | CSS *Skidgate* (buoy tender) | Canada[9] | Peter Kallis | East 6 |
| 15 | 1976 | CCGS *J. E. Bernier*[1] (icebreaker) | Canada[10] | Paul Pelland | East 3 |
| 16 | 1977 | *Williwaw* (13m sloop) | Netherlands | Willy de Roos | West 4 |
| | | *Single-handed after Gjøa Haven, continued to circumnavigate the Americas* | | | |
| 17 | 1978 | CCGS *Pierre Radisson* (icebreaker) | Canada[11] | Patrick R M Toomey | East 2 |
| 18 | 1976–9 | *J. E. Bernier II* (10m ketch) | Canada[12] | Réal Bouvier | West 4 |
| | | *Wintered in Holsteinborg, Resolute and Tuktoyaktuk* | | | |
| 19 | 1979 | Canmar Kigoriak (icebreaker) | Canada[13] | C Cunningham | West 2 |
| 20 | 1979 | CCGS *Louis S St Laurent* (icebreaker) | Canada[14] | George Burdock | West 2 |
| | | *Circumnavigated North America* | | | |
| 21 | 1980 | CCGS *J E Bernier*[2] (icebreaker) | Canada[15] | E Chasse | East 4 |
| 22 | 1980 | *Pandora II* (hydrographic survey vessel) | Canada[16] | R A Jones | East 4 |
| 23 | 1981 | CSS *Hudson*[2] (research icebreaker) | Canada[17] | F Mauger | East 3 |
| 24 | 1979–82 | *Mermaid* (15m sloop) | Japan | Kenichi Horie | West 6 |
| | | *First single-handed voyage, wintered in Resolute and Tuktoyaktuk* | | | |
| 25 | 1983 | *Arctic Shiko* (tug) | Canada[18] | S Dool | East 3 |
| 26 | 1983 | *Polar Circle* (research vessel) | Canada[10] | J A Strand | East 4 |
| 27 | 1984 | *Lindblad Explorer*[1] (ice-strengthened ship) | Sweden[1] | Hasse Nilsson | West 4 |
| | | *First passenger voyage* | | | |
| 28 | 1985 | USCGC *Polar Sea*[1] (icebreaker) | United States[5] | John T Howell | West 2 |
| | | *Accompanied by CCGS John A. McDonald for part of voyage* | | | |
| 29 | 1985 | *World Discoverer* (ice-strengthened ship) | Singapore | Heinz Aye[1] | East 4 |
| | | *Carried passengers*[2]*, traversed Pond Inlet* | | | |
| 30 | 1976–88 | *Canmar Explorer II* (drilling ship) | Canada[20] | Ronald Colby | West 3 |
| | | *Reached Beaufort Sea for oil-drilling programme from 1976 until completed transit* | | | |
| 31 | 1983–8 | *Belvedere* (18m yacht) | United States[6] | John Bockstoce | West 6 |
| | | *Reached Tuktoyaktuk 1983, conducted whaling research to 1987, completed transit in 1988, traversed Pond Inlet* | | | |
| 32 | 1985–8 | *Vagabond II*[1] (12·8m yacht) | France[1] | Janusz Kurbiel (1985–7) and Wojciech Jacobson (1988) | East 6 |
| | | *Wintered in Tuktoyaktuk and twice in Gjøa Haven (where changed masters), vessel circumnavigated North America* | | | |
| 33 | 1988 | CCGS *Henry A. Larsen* (icebreaker) | Canada[21] | Stephen Gomes | East 3 |
| 34 | 1988 | CCGS *Martha L Black* (icebreaker) | Canada[22] | Robert Mellis | East 3 |
| 35 | 1988 | USCGC *Polar Star*[1] (icebreaker) | United States[7] | Paul A Taylor | East 3 |
| | | *Accompanied by CCGS Sir John Franklin to Demarcation Point* | | | |
| 36 | 1988 | *Society Explorer*[2] (ice-strengthened ship) | Bahamas[1] | Heinz Aye[2] | East 3 |
| | | *Carried passengers*[3]*, traversed Pond Inlet [formerly Lindblad Explorer]* | | | |
| 37 | 1986-89 | *Mabel E Holland* (12·8m lifeboat) | Britain[1] | David Scott Cowper[1] | West 6 |
| | | *Single-handed voyage*[2]*, vessel wintered at Fort Ross (twice) and at Inuvik* | | | |

| | Year | Vessel | Registry | Master | Route |
|---|---|---|---|---|---|
| 38 | 1988-89 | *Northanger* (15m ketch) | Britain[2] | Richard Thomas | West 4 |
| | | | | | *Wintered in Inuvik* |
| 39 | 1989 | USCGC *Polar Star*[2] (icebreaker) | United States[8] | Robert Hammond | West 3 |
| | | | *Accompanied by CCGS Sir John Franklin to Demarcation Point* | | |
| 40 | 1983–90 | *Ikaluk*[1] (icebreaker) | Canada[23] | R Cormier[1] | East 3 |
| | | | *Reached Beaufort Sea in 1983, where worked to 1990 when completed transit* | | |
| 41 | 1990 | USCGC *Polar Sea*[2] (icebreaker) | United States[9] | Joseph J McClelland | West 3 |
| | | | *Accompanied by CCGS Pierre Radisson to Demarcation Point* | | |
| 42 | 1990 | *Terry Fox* (icebreaker) | Canada[24] | P Kimmerley | East 3 |
| 43 | 1991 | *Canmar Tugger* (tug) | Canada[25] | L. Lorengeek | East 3 |
| 44 | 1992 | *Frontier Spirit*[1] (ice-strengthened ship) | Bahamas[2] | Heinz Aye[3] | West 3 |
| | | | *Carried passengers[4], traversed Pond Inlet* | | |
| 45 | 1992 | *Ikaluk*[2] (icebreaker) | Canada[26] | R Cormier[2] | West 3 |
| 46 | 1992 | *Kapitan Khlebnikov*[1] (icebreaker) | Russia[1] | Piotr Golikov[1] | East 3 |
| | | | | | *Carried passengers[5]* |
| 47 | 1993 | *Frontier Spirit*[2] (ice-strengthened ship) | Bahamas[3] | Heinz Aye[4] | West 3 |
| 48 | 1993 | *Kapitan Khlebnikov*[2] (icebreaker) | Russia[2] | Piotr Golikov[2] | East 3 |
| | | | | | *Both carried passengers[6 & 7]* |
| 49 | 1993 | *Dagmar Aaen*[1] (27m yacht) | Germany[1] | Arved Fuchs | West 5 |
| 52 | 1994 | *Hanseatic*[1] (ice-strengthened ship) | Bahamas[4] | Hartwig van Harling[1] | West 3 |
| | | | | | *Carried passengers[8]* |
| 53 | 1994 | *Itasca* (converted tug) | Britain[3] | Allan Jouning | East 4 |
| 50 | 1994 | *Kapitan Khlebnikov*[3] (icebreaker) | Russia[3] | Piotr Golikov[3] | East 3 |
| 51 | 1994 | *Kapitan Khlebnikov*[4] (icebreaker) | Russia[4] | Piotr Golikov[4] | West 2 |
| | | | *Return voyage, carried passengers[9 & 10]* | | |
| 54 | 1995 | CCGS *Arctic Ivik*[1] (icebreaker) | Canada[27] | Norman Thomas | East 5 |
| 55 | 1995 | CCGS *Arctic Ivik*[2] (icebreaker) | Canada[28] | Robert Mellis | West 5 |
| | | | | | *Return voyage to and from Kap York* |
| 56 | 1995 | *Canmar Ikaluk*[3] (icebreaker) [formerly *Ikaluk*] | Canada[29] | D Connolly | East 3 |
| 57 | 1995 | *Canmar Miscaroo* (icebreaker) | Canada[30] | D W Harris | East 3 |
| 58 | 1995 | *Kapitan Khlebnikov*[5] (icebreaker) | Russia[5] | Viktor Vasiliev[1] | East 5 |
| | | | | | *Carried passengers[11]* |
| 59 | 1995 | *Dove III* (8·5m yacht) | Canada[31] | Winston Bushnell | East 3 |
| 60 | 1995 | *Hrvatska Cigra* [Croatian Tern] (19·8m yacht) | Croatia | Mladan Sutej | West 5 |
| 61 | 1996 | *Arctic Circle* (tug) | Canada[32] | Jack McCormack | East 3 |
| 62 | 1996 | *Canmar Supplier II* (cargo vessel) | Canada[33] | P Dunderdale | East 3 |
| 63 | 1996 | *Hanseatic*[2] (ice-strengthened ship) | Bahamas[5] | Hartwig van Harling[2] | West 3 |
| | | | *Carried passengers[12] until grounded in Simpson Strait, escorted by CCGS Henry A Larsen to Victoria Strait, traversed Pond Inlet* | | |
| 64 | 1996 | *Kapitan Dranitsyn*[1] (icebreaker) | Russia[6] | Oleg Agafonov | East 5 |
| | | | | | *Carried passengers[13]* |
| 65 | 1996 | CCGS *Sir Wilfrid Laurier* (icebreaker | Canada[34] | Norman Thomas | East 5 |
| | | | *Escorted by CCGS Louis S St Laurent for part of voyage, traversed Pond Inlet* | | |
| 66 | 1997 | *Alex Gordon* (tug) | Canada[35] | Paul Misata | East 5 |
| | | | *Escorted by CCGS Sir Wilfrid Laurier to Franklin Strait and then CCGS Pierre Radisson* | | |
| 67 | 1997 | *Hanseatic*[3] (ice-strengthened ship) | Bahamas[6] | Heinz Aye[5] | West 3 |
| | | | *Carried passengers[14], escorted to Victoria Strait by CCGS Henry A Larsen, traversed Pond Inlet* | | |
| 68 | 1997 | *Kapitan Khlebnikov*[6] (icebreaker) | Russia[7] | Viktor Vasiliev[2] | East 3 |
| | | | | | *Carried passengers[15]* |
| 69 | 1997 | *Supplier* (tug) | Bahamas[7] | Allan Guenter | East 5 |
| | | | | | *Escorted by CCGS Terry Fox to Victoria Strait* |
| 70 | 1998 | *Kapitan Khlebnikov*[7] (icebreaker) | Russia[8] | Piotr Golikov[5] | East 3 |
| | | | | | *Carried passengers[16]* |

| | Year | Vessel | Registry | Master | Route |
|---|---|---|---|---|---|
| 71 | 1998 | *Hanseatic[4]* (ice-strengthened ship) | Bahamas[8] | Heinz Aye[6] | East 3 |
| | | *Carried passengers[17], escorted to Victoria Strait by CCGS Sir John Franklin, traversed Pond Inlet* | | | |
| 72 | 1999 | *Admiral Makarov* (icebreaker, dock in tow) | Russia[9] | Vadim Kholodenko | East 3 |
| 73 | 1999 | *Irbis* (tug, dock in tow) | Russia[10] | Aleksandr Aleksenko | East 3 |
| | | *Travelled in convoy each towing a component of a steel floating dock, Korea to Caribbean* | | | |
| 74 | 1999 | *Kapitan Dranitsyn[2]* (icebreaker) | Russia[11] | Viktor Terekhov[1] | West 3 |
| | | *Carried passengers[18], circumnavigated the Arctic[1]* | | | |
| 75 | 1999 | *Ocean Search* (12·5m yacht) | France[2] | Olivier Pitras[1] | East 5 |
| | | *Traversed Pond Inlet* | | | |
| 76 | 2000 | *Hanseatic[5]* (ice-strengthened ship) | Bahamas[9] | Thilo Natke[1] | West 3 |
| | | *Carried passengers[19], traversed Pond Inlet* | | | |
| 77 | 2000 | USCGC *Healy[1]* (icebreaker) | United States[10] | Jeffrey M. Garrett | West 3 |
| 78 | 2000 | *Evohe* (25m yacht) | New Zealand[1] | Stephen Kafka | East 6 |
| 79 | 2000 | *Kapitan Dranitsyn[3]* (icebreaker) | Russia[12] | Viktor Terekhov[2] | West 3 |
| | | *Carried passengers[20], circumnavigated the Arctic[2]* | | | |
| 80 | 2000 | *Nadon [St Roch II]* (17·7m RCMP catamaran) | Canada[36] | Kenneth Burton | East 6 |
| | | *Voyage to commemorate St Roch 1940–2 transit* | | | |
| 81 | 2000 | *Simon Fraser* (icebreaker, formerly CCGS) | Canada[37] | Robert Mellis | East 6 |
| | | *Escorted Nadon* | | | |
| 82 | 2001 | *Kapitan Khlebnikov[8]* (icebreaker) | Russia[13] | Viktor Vasiliev[3] | East 3 |
| 83 | 2001 | *Kapitan Khlebnikov[9]* (icebreaker) | Russia[14] | Viktor Vasiliev[4] | West 1 |
| | | *Return voyage, carried passengers[21 & 22]* | | | |
| 84 | 2001 | *Northabout* (14·9m yacht) | Ireland (Éire) | Jarlath Cunnane | West 4 |
| | | *Circumnavigated the Arctic[3]* | | | |
| 85 | 2001 | *Turmoil* (46m yacht) | Cayman Islands[1] | Philip Walsh | West 4 |
| | | *Traversed Pond Inlet* | | | |
| 86 | 2001-02 | *Nuage* (12·8m yacht) | France[3] | Michèle Demai | East 3 |
| | | *Complement of mother and daughter, wintered in Cambridge Bay* | | | |
| 87 | 2002 | *Apostol Andrey* (16·2m yacht) | Russia[15] | Nikolay Litau | East 5 |
| | | *Assisted by CCGS Louis S St Laurent through Prince Regent Inlet, circumnavigated the Arctic[4]* | | | |
| 88 | 2002 | *Arctic Kalvik* (icebreaker tug) | Barbados | Sanjeev Kumar | East 3 |
| 89 | 2002 | *Hanseatic[6]* (ice-strengthened ship) | Bahamas[10] | Thilo Natke[2] | West 3 |
| | | *Carried passengers[23], traversed Pond Inlet* | | | |
| 90 | 2002 | *Kapitan Khlebnikov[10]* (icebreaker) | Russia[16] | Piotr Golikov[1] | East 3 |
| | | *Carried passengers[24]* | | | |
| 91 | 2002 | *Sedna IV* (51m yacht) | Canada[38] | Stéphan Guy | West 5 |
| 92 | 2003 | *Kapitan Khlebnikov[11]* (icebreaker) | Russia[17] | Viktor Vasiliev[5] | East 5 |
| 93 | 2003 | *Bremen[3]* (ice-strengthened ship) | Bahamas[11] | Daniel Felgner | West 3 |
| | | *Both carried passengers[25 & 26], Bremen [formerly Frontier Spirit] traversed Pond Inlet* | | | |
| 94 | 2003 | USCGC *Healy[2]* (icebreaker) | United States[11] | Daniel Oliver | West 3 |
| 95 | 2003 | *Norwegian Blue* (12·9m yacht) | Britain[4] | Andrew Wood | East 5 |
| 96 | 2003 | *Vagabond[2]* (15·3m yacht) | France[4] | Eric Brossier | East 5 |
| | | *Both traversed Pond Inlet; Vagabond [formerly Vagabond II] circumnavigated the Arctic[5]* | | | |
| 97 | 2003–4 | *Dagmar Aaen[2]* (27m yacht) | Germany[2] | Arved Fuchs[2] | East 5 |
| | | *Wintered in Cambridge Bay, traversed Pond Inlet; circumnavigated the Arctic[6]* | | | |
| 98 | 2003–4 | *Polar Bound[1]* (14·6m motorboat) | Britain[5] | David Scott Cowper[2] | West 5 |
| | | *Single-handed voyage[3], wintered in Cambridge Bay, assisted by CCGS Louis S St Laurent in Prince Regent Inlet* | | | |
| 99 | 2003-06 | *Minke I* (12·8m yacht) | Canada[40] | Peter Brook | East 6 |
| | | *Wintered in Tuktoyaktuk and in Cambridge Bay twice* | | | |
| 100 | 2004 | *Kapitan Khlebnikov[12]* (icebreaker) | Russia[18] | Pavel Ankudinov[1] | East 5 |
| | | *Carried passengers[27]* | | | |

| | Year | Vessel | Registry | Master | Route |
|---|---|---|---|---|---|
| 101 | 2004-05 | *Fine Tolerance* (13·7m yacht) | Australia1 | Philip Hogg | East 6 |
| | | *Wintered in Cambridge Bay, assisted by CCGS Sir Wilfrid Laurier and CCGS Louis S St Laurent through Bellot Strait* | | | |
| 102 | 2005 | *Kapitan Khlebnikov*[13] (icebreaker) | Russia[19] | Viktor Vasiliev[6] | East 3 |
| 103 | 2005 | *Kapitan Khlebnikov*[14] (icebreaker) | Russia[20] | Viktor Vasiliev[7] | West 3 |
| | | *Carried passengers[28] on eastbound voyage* | | | |
| 104 | 2005 | *Idlewild* (17·3m motorboat) | Canada[39] | Benjamin Grey | East 6 |
| | | *Assisted by CCGS Sir Wilfrid Laurier and CCGS Louis S St Laurent through Bellot Strait* | | | |
| 105 | 2005 | *Oden* (icebreaker) | Sweden[2] | Anders Wikström | West 3 |
| 106 | 2006 | *Kapitan Khlebnikov*[15] (icebreaker) | Russia[21] | Pavel Ankudinov[2] | East 7 |
| | | *Carried passengers[29]* | | | |
| 107 | 2006 | *Nekton* (13·6m yacht) | Poland[1] | Tadeusz Natenek | East 4 |
| 108 | 2006 | *Stary* (13·5m yacht) | Poland[2] | Dominik Bak, Jacek Waclawski and Slawek Skalmierski | East 4 |
| | | *Travelled in company, traversed Pond Inlet (Stary changed masters at Cambridge Bay and Tuktoyaktuk)* | | | |
| 109 | 2007 | *Babouche* (7·5m catamaran) | France[5] | Sébastien Roubinet | East 5 |
| 110 | 2007 | *Cloud Nine* (17·3m ketch) | United States[12] | Roger Swanson | West 4 |
| 111 | 2007 | *Hanseatic*[7] (ice-strengthened ship) | Bahamas[12] | Ulf Wolter[1] | West 5 |
| 112 | 2007 | *Kapitan Khlebnikov*[16] (icebreaker) | Russia[22] | Viktor Vasiliev[8] | East 5 |
| | | *Both carried passengers[30 & 31]* | | | |
| 113 | 2007 | *Luck Dragon* (12·1m yacht) | Britain[6] | Jeffrey Allison | West 3 |
| | | *Vessel abandoned during a storm in Bering Sea* | | | |
| 114 | 2005–8 | *Arctic Wanderer* (11·9m yacht) | United States[13] | Gary E. Ramos | East 6 |
| | | *Single-handed voyage[4], wintered three times in Cambridge Bay* | | | |
| 115 | 2008 | *Bremen*[4] (ice-strengthened ship) | Bahamas[13] | Ulf Wolter[2] | West 5 |
| | | *Carried passengers[32]* | | | |
| 116 | 2008 | *Amodino* (23m yacht) | New Zealand[2] | Juan Ribos | West 4 |
| 117 | 2008 | *Baloum Gwen*[1] (14·9m yacht) | Belgium[1] | Thierry Fabing[1] | West 4 |
| 118 | 2008 | *Berrimilla* (10m yacht) | Australia[2] | Alexander Whitworth | East 4 |
| 119 | 2008 | *Geraldine* (14m yacht) | United States[14] | Walter Jones | West 3 |
| 120 | 2008 | *Southern Star* (23·7m yacht) | France[6] | Olivier Pitras[2] | West 4 |
| 121 | 2008 | *Tyhina* (10·4m yacht) | New Zealand[3] | Peter Elliott | West 4 |
| 122 | 2009 | *Apoise* (67m motor vessel) | Canada[41] | David Ritchie | West 4 |
| 123 | 2009 | *Bagan* (17·4m motorboat) | United States[15] | Clinton Bolton | West 4 |
| 124 | 2009 | *Bremen*[5] (ice-strengthened ship) | Bahamas[14] | Marc Behrend | West 4 |
| | | *Carried passengers[33], traversed Pond Inlet* | | | |
| 125 | 2009 | *Baloum Gwen*[2] (14·9m yacht) | Belgium[2] | Thierry Fabing[2] | East 6 |
| | | *Return voyage* | | | |
| 126 | 2009 | *Fleur Australe* (20m yacht) | France[7] | Philippe Poupon | West 4 |
| 127 | 2009 | *Fiona* (12·8m yacht) | United States[16] | Eric Forsyth | West 4 |
| 128 | 2009 | *Glory of the Sea* (15·3m yacht) | France[8] | Charles Hedrich | West 4 |
| 129 | 2009 | *Hanseatic*[8] (ice-strengthened ship) | Bahamas[15] | Thilo Natke[3] | East 4 |
| | | *Carried passengers[34], voyage included a return transit of Bellot Strait from Peel Sound* | | | |
| 130 | 2009 | *Ocean Watch* (19·2m yacht) | United States[17] | Mark Schrader | East 6 |
| 131 | 2009 | *Perithia* (14·6m yacht) | Germany[3] | Uwe Wohnort | West 4 |
| 132 | 2009 | *Polar Bound*[2] (14·6m motorboat) | Britain[7] | David Scott Cowper[3] | West 5 |
| | | *Single-handed voyage[5]* | | | |
| 133 | 2009 | *Precipice* (9·1m yacht) | United States[18] | Rolland Trowbridge | West 6 |
| 134 | 2009 | *Silent Sound* (12·2m yacht) | Canada[42] | Cameron Dueck | East 6 |
| | | *Traversed Pond Inlet* | | | |
| 135 | 2010 | *Ariel IV* (15·2m sloop) | Sweden[3] | Eric Boye | West 4 |
| 136 | 2010 | *Astral Express* (12·5m yacht) | New Zealand[4] | Graeme Kendall | West 3 |

| | Year | Vessel | Registry | Master | Route |
|---|---|---|---|---|---|
| 137 | 2010 | *Hanseatic*[9] (ice-strengthened ship) | Bahamas[16] | Ulf Wolter[3] | West 4 |
| | | | | *Carried passengers[35], traversed Pond Inlet* | |
| 138 | 2010 | *Kapitan Khlebnikov*[17] (icebreaker) | Russia[23] | Anatoliy Kovalenko | East 5 |
| | | | | | *Carried passengers[36]* |
| 139 | 2010 | *Octopus* (128m motor yacht) | Cayman Islands[2] | Jannek Olsson | East 2 |
| | | | | | *Traversed Pond Inlet* |
| 140 | 2010 | *Rx II* (11m yacht) | Norway[2] | Trond Aasvoll | East 4 |
| 141 | 2010 | *Sarema* (15·2m yacht) | Finland | Pekka Kauppila | East 4 |
| | | | | | *Traversed Pond Inlet* |
| 142 | 2010 | *Solanus* (14·5m yacht) | Poland[3] | Bronislaw Radlinski | West 4 |
| 143 | 2010 | *Young Larry* (13·4m yacht) | Britain[8] | Andrew Wilkes | West 4 |
| 144 | 2010-11 | *Anna* (10·5m ketch) | Sweden[4] | Börje Ivarsson | West 4 |
| | | | | | *Wintered in Inuvik* |
| 145 | 2011 | *Arcadia* (35·8m motor yacht) | Cayman Islands[3] | James Pizzaruso | West 5 |
| | | | | | *Traversed Pond Inlet* |
| 146 | 2011 | *Asteria* (converted tug) | Marshall Islands | Donald Feil | West 3 |
| 147 | 2011 | *Bremen*[6] (ice-strengthened ship) | Bahamas[17] | Marc Behrend[2] | East 1, 2, 4 |
| | | *Composite course: McClure Strait, Prince of Wales Strait and then route 4; carried passengers[37]* | | | |
| 148 | 2011 | *Chamade* (13·3m yacht) | Switzerland | Marc Decrey | West 4 |
| 149 | 2011 | *Essamy* (15·5m yacht) | Britain[9] | Jeffrey Allison | West 5 |
| 150 | 2011 | *Imvubu* (15·9m ketch) | South Africa | Ralf Dominick | West 3 |
| 151 | 2011 | *Issuma* (15m schooner) | Canada[43] | Richard Hudson | West 5 |
| 152 | 2011 | *Kotuku* (12·2m yacht) | New Zealand[5] | Ian Jefferies | East 5 |
| 153 | 2011 | *Leavre* (12·5m sloop) | France[9] | Not known | East 5 |
| 154 | 2011 | *Muktuk* (14·3m sloop) | Austria | Karl Mayer | West 4 |
| 155 | 2011 | *Pangaeas* (35m yacht) | United States[19] | Michael Horn | East 4 |
| 156 | 2011 | *Polar Bound*[2] (14·6 m. motorboat) | Britain[10] | David Scott Cowper[4] | East 3 |
| 157 | 2011 | *Roxane* (10·7m sloop) | France[10] | Luc Dupont | West 4 |
| 158 | 2011 | *Rus* (7·6m trimaran) | Russia[24] | Oleg Volynkin | West 4 |
| 159 | 2011 | *St Brendan* (8·2m yacht) | United States[20] | Matt Rutherford | West 3 |
| 160 | 2011 | *Santa Maria Australis* (20·1m ketch) | Germany[4] | Wolf Kloss | West 4 |

*Transit 151,*
*schooner* **Issuma**
*in the Passage.*

# SELECTED REFERENCES

Amundsen, Roald *The North West Passage*, Constable 1908

*Arctic Canada, Sailing Directions*, Dept. of Fisheries Ottawa 2011

*Arctic Pilot* vol. 3, UK Hydrographic Office 2007

Belcher, Captain Sir Edward *The Last of the Arctic Voyages*, London 1855

Bockstoce, John R *Furs and Frontiers in the Far North*, Yale University Press 2009

Davis, John *The Seaman's Secrets*, 1594

Delgado, James *Across the Top of the World*, Douglas & McIntyre 2009

Fleming, Fergus *Barrow's Boys*, Granta Books 1999

Grant, Shelagh *Polar Imperative: Arctic Sovereignty in North America*, Douglas & McIntyre 2010

*Guidelines for the Operation of Passenger Vessels*, Transport Canada 2005

Hayes, Derek *Historical Atlas of the Arctic*, Vancouver 2003

Headland, R K 'Ten Decades of Transits', *Polar Geography*, 33: 1, 1-13 2010

McClure, Robert *The Discovery of a North-west Passage*, London 1857

Parry, William Edward *Journals*, London 1821–8

Rasmussen, Knut *Across Arctic America*, Putnam 1927

Ross, John *A Voyage of Discovery* John Murray 1819

Ross, Sir John *In Search of a North-West Passage*, London 1835

Savours, Ann *The Search for the North West Passage*, Chatham 1999

Scoresby, William *An Account of the Arctic Regions*, Constable 1820

Smith, Jared *The New North*, Profile 2011

Soper, Tony *The Arctic – Coastal Wildlife*, Bradt 2012

Soublière, Marion *The Nunavut Handbook*, Iqaluit 2004

Williams, Glyn *Arctic Labyrinth*, Allen Lane 2009

# ICE INFORMATION

*Canadian Ice Service charts* www.ice-glaces.ec.gc.ca

*National Snow & Ice Data Center* www.nsidc.org

*University of Bremen Polarview* www.polarview.org/services/ gsim.htm

*US National Ice Centre* www.nsidc.org/arcticseaicenews

# EXPEDITION OPERATORS

*Adventure Canada* www.adventurecanada.com

*EYOS Expeditions* www.eyos-expeditions.com

*Hapag-Lloyd Cruises* www.hl-cruises.com

*Lindblad Expeditions* www.expeditions.com

*One Ocean Expeditions* www.oneoceanexpeditions.com

*Quark Expeditions* www.quarkexpeditions.com

# ACKNOWLEDGEMENTS

As colleagues on half a dozen transits of the Northwest Passage I owe huge debts to historian Bob Headland of the Scott Polar Research Institute, geologist/botanist Norm Lasca of the University of Milwaukee and ornithologist Roger Lovegrove. Ice Pilot Captain Pat Toomey of the Canadian Coastguard improved my understanding of ice navigation. Captains Victor Vasiliev and Pavel Ankudinov of the icebreaker *Kapitan Khlebnikov* avoided the worst of the ice and carried us with aplomb in the wake of Edward Parry and Roald Amundsen; but it was Lars and Erica Wikander of Quark Expeditions who hired us to enjoy the spectacular scenery and wildlife of the archipelago. I explored the Bering Sea with Captain Thilo Natke in Hapag-Lloyd's elegant *Hanseatic*. Andrew Prossin of One Ocean Expeditions and Matthew Swan of Adventure Canada found me berths in the ice-hardened research vessels *Akademik Ioffe* and *Professor Multanovskiy* and I warmly appreciated their generosity. Sailing with the historian Peter Irniq was a much-needed education in Inuit history. And three cheers for the Kingsbridge branch of Devon County Library.

TS

**www.tonysoper.com**

# PHOTOGRAPHIC ACKNOWLEDGEMENTS

The authors and publishers are grateful to the following for permission to reproduce copyright images:

Tips Images (©Andy Stewart) i; Hilary Emberton iii, vi, 42, 44, 46b, 51, 52, 53, 63, 71, 96, 123; Martin Enckell 2, 4, 66, 70, 97, 124, 135, 137; Tony Soper 3, 54, 57, 61, 68, 80, 88, 89, 90, 133, 136, 140; Peter Puleston (illustration by the late Dennis Puleston) 12; Patrick Toomey 35; Vancouver Maritime Museum 39; Lindblad Expeditions 41; Shutterstock 46a (©Pavel Svoboda), 50 (© Francis Bossé), 84 (© Dennis Donohue), 86 (© Elliotte Rusty Harold), 100 (© Richard Seeley), 111 (© Delmas Lehman); Brandon Harvey 49, 55, 59, 62, 75, 85, 92, 95, 104, 129, 154; Keith Shackleton 69; Daniel Georg Nyblin/National Library of Norway, bldsa–NBRA0005 79; Tui De Roy/Minden Pictures/FLPA 83; © Johner Images/Alamy 102; Woods Hole Oceanographic Institution 107; Tony Martin 114, 115, Tony Beck 120, 121, (c) Robert Postma/All Canada Photos/Corbis 131; Ralf Dominick 149

Other sources: page 6 Sir William Jardine, *The Naturalist's Library*, 1839; 8 Cornelis Ketel, 1577; 10 Theodore de Bry, 1596; 14 Thomas James, *The Strange and Dangerous Voyage*, 1631; 15 View of Snug Corner Cove, John Webber, 1778 ; 17 Sir Joshua Reynolds, 1773; 18 Captain John Ross, *A Voyage of Discovery*, 1819; 19 W E Parry, *Journals*, 1821–28; 21 E Finden, 1833; 25 Samuel Gurney Cresswell, 1853; 27 Captain Sir Edward Belcher, 1852; 28 Punch, 13 December 1856; 29 Illustrated London News, 4 November 1854; 30 Lithograph of Jane, Lady Franklin, by Joseph Negelen, after a drawing by Amélie Romilly); 36 Roald Amundsen; 38 C L Andrews, 1906; 45 Sir William Jardine *The Naturalist's Library* 1839; 99 George Back, 1821; 122 Sir William Jardine *The Naturalist's Library* 1839.

For more detailed mapping than has been possible in this book, please see the Canadian Hydrographic Service's chart 7000.

Every effort has been made to track down copyright holders for material used in this book; the publishers apologise for any omissions and will be pleased to make appropriate acknowledgement in any future editions.

## About the author

As expedition leader and wildlife lecturer, Tony Soper has circumnavigated the Arctic coast by both the Northeast and Northwest Passages and reached the North Pole four times by icebreaker.

# INDEX

Main entries are in **bold**, illustrations in *italic*

Adolphus, Prince 87
Amundsen, Roald **36,** 64,
  79, **139**
  in Gjoa Haven 78
Archaeological Service 35
Arctic Squadron 26, *27*
Auks **66**
Aulavik NP 111
Austin, Horatio 26, 62

Back, George 81
Baffin, William 13
Banks Island 25
Banks, Joseph 16, *17*, 110
Barrow **132**
Barrow, John 16, 32
Basin, Rasmussen 80
Basque whalers 5
Bay, Arctic 52
  Baffin 37, 43
  Cambridge **87,** *88*
  Croker **57**
  Darnley 105
  Franklin 108
  Frobisher 47
  Johansen 96
  Mercy 25, 35
  Prudhoe **132**
  Radstock 58
  Resolute 63
  Spence 77
Bear, Grizzly **100**
  hybrid 112
Bear, Polar *4*, **60**
Beattie, Professor Owen
  32
Beechey, Frederick William
  18
Belcher, Edward 26
Bellot, Joseph 62, 72
Beluga **114**
Bering, Vitus 15, 138
Bird, Edward 24
Bloody Falls Park 98
Bonaparte, Napoleon 16
Boundary, Yukon/Alaska
  130
Brabant, Port 116
Braine, William 26
Bunting, Lapland 49
  Snow **50**
Bylot, Robert 13

Cabot, John 7
  Sebastian 7
Cannibalism 29
Cape Dezhnev 138
  Dorset 54
  Felix 78
  Parry 106
  Prince of Wales 138

Caribou, barren-ground **94**
  porcupine 131
Cartier, Jacques 15
Caswell Tower 58
Cathay Company 8
Channel, Parry 52, 63
  Wellington 32, 58, 62
Church, Roman Catholic
  106
CLAMER 113
Collinson, Richard 25
Columbus, Christopher 7
Cook, James 15
Cresswell, Samuel Gurney
  25, *25*
Croker, John Wilson 17,
  57
Crozier, Francis 22, 31
Culture, Thule 45, 119
  Dorset 45
Curragh 5

Date Line, International
  135
Davis, John 8ff
Divers **132**
Dorset culture 45
Duck, long-tailed **86**
Dundas Harbour 54
Eagle, Alaska 37
Eskimos, Copper 101
EYOS Expeditions 42

Fitzjames, James 31
Fort Ross 71
Fox, Arctic **128**
Foxe, Luke 13
Franklin, John 19, 59, **22**,
  31, 119
Franklin, Jane, Lady 30,
  *30*, 102
Frobisher, Martin 8

Gall, Scotty 73
Gjoa Haven 78
Goose, Canada **84**
  Snow 82, **111**
Grenier, Robert 33
Guillemot, Black 126
  Brünnich's 65
Gulf, Amundsen 101
  Queen Maud 35, **81**
Gull, glaucous **68**
  ivory **70**
  Ross's 135, **136**
  Sabine's 135, **136**
Gyrfalcon **69**

Haakon VII, King 38
*Hanseatic 42*
Hansen, Godfred 37

Hanssen, Helmer, 37
Harbour, Baychimo 93
  Craig 56
  Dundas 54
  Sachs **110**
  Victory 21
Hare, Arctic 53
Hartnell, John 26
Haven, Gjoa 37, **78**
Headland, Robert 42, 141
Herschel, John 119
Hills, Smoking 108
Holman **102**
Holman, J R 102
Hudson's Bay Company
  54, 73
Huskies 45

Ice, sea 76
Ikahuak 110
Ikaluktutiak 87
Ikpiarjuk 51
Inglefield, Edward 102
Inlet, Admiralty 51
  Bathurst **93**
  Chantrey **82**
  Navy Board 51
  Pond **48,** *48*
  Prince Regent 70
Inuit 44, 45, 47,
  Copper 101
Inuksuk *92*
Inuktituk 47
Iqaluit 47
*Isabella 21*, 48
Island, Baffin 54
  Banks 35
  Beechey 25, 32, **59**
  Cornwallis 32
  Devon 26, 53
  Halfway 73
  Herschel 37, **118**
  King William 29, 32, **78**
  Melville 25
  Prince Leopold 65
  *Issuma*, Sloop *149*

James, Thomas 14, *14*
Joss, Billy 104

*Kapitan Khlebnikov,*
  icebreaker *3, 140,* 143
Kayaks 45
Kellett, Henry 24, 27
Kennedy, William 72
Kimaqtut 102
Kittiwake, Black-legged **56**
Kotzebue, Otto von 15
Kugluktuk **98**

Land bridge, Bering 5
Lemming, collared **107**

Lindstrøm, Adolf 37
Longitude, Board of 16
Loon 133
Lund, Anton 37
Lyon, George 19

Manhattan, SS 40
Mason, Fortnum and 23
McClintock, Francis 27, 31
McClure, Robert 16, 25, 27, 109
Memorial, Franklin 62
Merchant Venturers, Bristol 13
Mittimatalik 48
Moore, Thomas 24
Mountains, Croker 16, 17
Murre, thick-billed 65
Muscovy Company 8, 13
Museum, Fram 38
  Prince of Wales 62

Nanisivik 52
Nanuk 60
Narwhal 74
Nationalism, Norwegian 37
Nilsson, Hasse 41
Nome 38
Nordenskjold, Adolf 36
Northern Transportation Co. 4, 117
Northumberland House 62, 63
Nunavut 43

Ommaney, Erasmus 26
Oscar, King 37
Ox, musk 55, 112

Paleo-Eskimo people 44
Panama Canal 1, 2
Parry, William Edward 17, 59, 137
Paulatuk 105
Peninsula, Chukotka 135
Phalarope, grey 89

Pigniq archaeological site 134
Pingo National Landmark 117
Piqiarniq 47
Poisoning, lead 33
Pole, North 41
  North Magnetic 77
Police, RCM 39, 54, 123
Politics 3
Pond Inlet 48, 48
Pond, John 48
Pullen, W J S 62

Qaliujaaqpait 47
Qausuittuq 63
Qikiqtaruq 118
Qingaun 93

Rae, Dr John 28
Rasmussen, Knut 39
Raven 49
Region, Inuvik 102
Resolute 63
Resolute 27
Ristveldt, Peder 37
River, Back 81
  Coppermine 19, 98, 99
  Mackenzie 127
  Porcupine 127
Ross, Fort 71
Ross, James Clark 24. 48, 58, 136
Ross, John 17ff
Route, Northern 6

Sagavanirktok 132
St Roch, schooner 39, 39
Saxifrage, Alpine 96
Scoresby, William 16
Sea, Beaufort 41, 113
  Bering 138
  Chukchi 15, 135
Seal, ringed 82
Shackleton, Keith 69
Sirmilik National Park 52
Skuas 97
Smoking Hills 108

Sound, Cumberland 11
  Lancaster 17, 26, 53
  Larsen 77
  Peel 32, 65
Sovereignty, Canadian 40
Squadron, Arctic 26, 27
Steele, George P. 41
Stefansson, Vilhjamur 101
Strait, Bellot 72
  Bering 15, 138
  Dolphin and Union 99
  Franklin 76
  James Ross 77
  Simpson 81
  Victoria 32, 35, 77

Talluriti 54
Talyoak 77
Tariunnuaq 81
Tern, Arctic 90
Terrible, Ivan the 8
Thule culture 45, 54, 119
Times, The 38
Torrington, John 26
Tower, Caswell 58
Transits 141
Tuktoyaktuk 116
Tuktuk Nogait NP 106
Tundra, Arctic 126

Ukpeagvik 132
Ulu 102
Ulukhaktok 102
Umiaks 45
Umingmaktok 93
Upsuqtuuq 78

Victoria, Queen 28, 28
Victory 20

Walrus 124
Walsingham, Francis 9
Wars, Napoleonic 16
Whale, Beluga 114
  Bowhead 6, 119, 120
Whalers 5, 6, 9, 23, 117, 119, 119, 134
Wiik, Gustav 37
Wildlife Refuge 130

Yukon 130